THIRD EDITION

BOOK 4

Steven J. Molinsky
Bill Bliss

Illustrated by

Richard E. Hill

Longman

longman.com

Side by Side, 3rd edition
Student Book 4

Pearson Education, 10 Bank Street, White Plains, NY 10606

Vice president, director of publishing: *Allen Ascher*
Editorial director: *Pam Fishman*
Vice president, director of design and production: *Rhea Banker*
Director of electronic production: *Aliza Greenblatt*
Production manager: *Ray Keating*
Director of manufacturing: *Patrice Fraccio*
Digital layout specialist: *Wendy Wolf*
Associate art director: *Elizabeth Carlson*
Interior design: *Elizabeth Carlson, Wendy Wolf*
Cover design: *Elizabeth Carlson*
Copyediting: *Janet Johnston*

Contributing *Side by Side* Gazette authors: *Laura English, Meredith Westfall*

Photo credits: p. 47, (*top, right*) ©CORBIS, (*top, left*) ©CORBIS, (*center, right*) Hulton Archive/Getty Images Inc., (*center, left*) ©Bettmann/CORBIS, (*bottom, right*) ©Bettmann/CORBIS, (*bottom, left*) ©Bettmann/CORBIS; p. 48, 1st row: (*left*) David Sutherland/Getty Images Inc., (*center*) H.H./Getty Images Inc., (*right*) Mahaux Photography/Getty Images Inc., 2nd row: (*left*) ©Roger Ressmeyer/CORBIS, (*center*) ©Brian A. Vikander/CORBIS, (*right*) ©David G. Houser/CORBIS, 3rd row: (*left*) Travel Pix/Getty Images Inc., (*center*) ©Charles & Josette Lenars/CORBIS, (*right*) ©Danny Lehman/CORBIS; p. 49, G & M David deLossy/Getty Images Inc.; p. 79, 1st row: (*left*) Photofest, (*right*) Bill Steber/Getty Images Inc., 2nd row: (*left*) Photofest, (*right*) Movie Still Archives, 3rd row: (*left*) Troy Augusto/Getty Images Inc. (*right*) ©Bettmann/CORBIS, 4th row: ©Neal Preston/CORBIS; p. 80, 1st row: (*left*) Robin Smith/Getty Images Inc., (*center*) Ken Ross/Getty Images Inc., (*right*) SW Productions/Getty Images Inc./PhotoDisc, Inc., 2nd row: (*left*) Yellow Dog Productions/Getty Images Inc., (*right*) Tom Campbell/Index Stock Imagery, Inc., 3rd row: (*left*) SuperStock, Inc., (*center*) Thierry Dosogne/Getty Images Inc., (*right*) Peter Turner/Getty Images Inc., 4th row: (*left*) Yellow Dog Productions/Getty Images Inc., (*right*) Dia Max/Getty Images Inc., 5th row: (*left*) ©Michael Busselle/CORBIS, (*right*) Max Dunning/Michael Dannenbaum/Getty Images Inc.; p. 81, (*left*) ©Walter Hodges/CORBIS, (*top, left*) ©R.W. Jones/CORBIS, (*top, center*) Larry Dale Gordon/Getty Images Inc., (*top, right*) Don Bonsey/Getty Images Inc., (*bottom, left*) Britt Erlanson/Getty Images Inc., (*bottom, center*) Jim Cummins/Getty Images Inc., (*bottom, right*) Stephen Simpson/Getty Images Inc.; p. 125, Don Klumpp/Getty Images Inc.; p. 126, (*top, left*) Bob Daemmrich/The Image Works, (*top, right*) Jean Luc Morales/Getty Images Inc., (*bottom, left*) Miao China Tourism Press/Wang/Getty Images Inc., (*bottom, center*) Francisco Cruz/SuperStock, Inc., (*bottom, right*) AJA Productions/Getty Images Inc.; p. 127, SuperStock, Inc.; p. 159, (*top, left*) ©Bettmann/CORBIS, (*top, right*) ©Ariel Skelley/CORBIS, (*bottom, left*) ©Bettmann/CORBIS, (*bottom, right*) ©Jon Feingersh/CORBIS/Stock market; p. 160, 1st row: (*left*) John Chiasson/Liaison/Getty Images Inc., (*right*) Fujifotos/Yoshida/The image Works, 2nd row: (*left*) AP/World Wide Photos, (*right*) Dan Connell/The Image Works, 3rd row: (*left*) John Maier, Jr/The Image Works, (*right*) Pascal Volery/Reuters/Getty Images Inc., 4th row: (*left*) ©F. Carter Smith/CORBIS/SYGMA, (*right*) ©Walter Hodges/CORBIS; p. 161, (*left*) David Young-Wolff/PhotoEdit, (*top, left*) ©Steve Chenn/CORBIS, (*top, center*) AP/World Wide Photos, (*top, right*) ©Bill Schild/CORBIS, (*bottom, left*) Larry Dale Gordon/Getty Images Inc., (*bottom, center*) Tony Freeman/PhotoEdit, (*bottom, right*) ©Ralph White/CORBIS.

The authors gratefully acknowledge the contribution
of Tina Carver in the development of the original
Side by Side program.

ISBN 0-13-026888-7   (Regular Edition)

10 – RRD – 13 12 11 10 09

ISBN 0-13-184180-7   (Student Book with Audio Highlights)

7 8 9 10 11 – RRD – 13 12 11 10 09

ISBN 0-13-183937-3   (International Edition)

8 9 10 11 12 13 14 – RRD – 14 13 12 11 10 09 08   Printed in the United States of America

CONTENTS

Review:
Present Perfect Tense
Present Perfect Continuous Tense
Past Perfect Tense
Past Perfect Continuous Tense

- Describing Actions That Have Occurred
- Describing Actions That Haven't Occurred Yet
- Discussing Duration of Activity
- Discussing Things People Had Done

VOCABULARY PREVIEW

Things to Do Today

☐ 1. take inventory

☐ 2. write a report

☐ 3. speak to the boss

☐ 4. go to the bank

☐ 5. eat lunch

☐ 6. give out the paychecks

☐ 7. set up the meeting room

☐ 8. see the personnel officer

☐ 9. get gas

☐ 10. drive to the gym

☐ 11. swim

☐ 12. do sit-ups

Things I've Done Today: I've . . .

☑ **1.** taken inventory
☑ **2.** written a report
☑ **3.** spoken to the boss
☑ **4.** gone to the bank

☑ **5.** eaten lunch
☑ **6.** given out the paychecks
☑ **7.** set up the meeting room
☑ **8.** seen the personnel officer

☑ **9.** gotten gas
☑ **10.** driven to the gym
☑ **11.** swum
☑ **12.** done sit-ups

I've Sung for Many Years

(I have)	I've
(We have)	We've
(You have)	You've
(They have)	They've
(He has)	He's
(She has)	She's
(It has)	It's

⎫ eaten.

A. Can you sing?

B. Yes. I've sung for many years.

1. *swim*
   swum

2. *draw pictures*
   drawn

3. *drive trucks*
   driven

4. *speak French*
   spoken

5. *fly airplanes*
   flown

6. *take inventory*
   taken

7. *grow corn*
   grown

8. *ride horses*
   ridden

9. *write speeches*
   written

Have You Eaten Lunch Yet?

Have	I we you they	eaten?
Has	he she it	

Yes,	I we you they	have.
	he she it	has.

eat
ate
eaten

A. Have you **eaten** lunch yet?

B. Yes, I have. I **ate** lunch a little while ago.

write
wrote
written

A. Has Tina **written** her composition yet?

B. Yes, she has. She **wrote** her composition a little while ago.

---

go
went
gone

1. *you*
go to the post office

give
gave
given

2. *Dan*
give out the paychecks

take
took
taken

3. *you and Susan*
take a break

do
did
done

4. *you*
do Room 24

see
saw
seen

5. *the employees*
see the new copy machine

feed
fed
fed

6. *Michael*
feed the monkeys

No, They Haven't

Have	I we you they	eaten?
Has	he she it	

No,	I we you they	haven't.
	he she it	hasn't.

I We You They	haven't (have not)	eaten.
He She It	hasn't (has not)	

give
gave
given

give blood

A. Have you **given** blood recently?

B. No, I haven't. I haven't **given** blood in a long time.

go
went
gone

go fishing

A. Has your father **gone** fishing recently?

B. No, he hasn't. He hasn't **gone** fishing in a long time.

write
wrote
written

1. *you*
   write in your journal

be
was/were
been

2. *Dorothy*
   be sick

get
got
gotten

3. *your son*
   get a haircut

run
ran
run

4. *you and your wife*
   run in a marathon

have
had
had .

5. *you*
   have a medical checkup

wear
wore
worn

6. *Anthony*
   wear his tuxedo

How Long?

for	since
five years	five o'clock
a week	last week
a long time	2001
many years	he started college

A. How long have you known how to water-ski?

B. I've known how to water-ski for many years.

A. How long has Alexander been a vegetarian?

B. He's been a vegetarian since he started college.

1. *be married*
   ten years

2. *have a toothache*
   ten o'clock this morning

3. *be in the hospital*
   last week

4. *own this car*
   thirty-two years

5. *have a British accent*
   she moved to London

6. *know each other*
   2001

7. *play the violin*
   he was in first grade

8. *like hip hop music*
   a long time

9. *want to be an actress*
   she was four years old

READING

A VERY BUSY DAY AT THE OFFICE

Things to Do Today

- ☑ go to the bank
- ☐ take the mail to the post office
- ☐ write my monthly report
- ☑ meet with the personnel officer about my maternity leave
- ☐ speak to the boss about my salary
- ☑ send a fax to the company's office in Tokyo
- ☐ read the office manager's memo about recycling
- ☐ see the training video about the new computer system

Allison is having a very busy day at the office. She has done some of the things she has to do today, but there are many other things she hasn't done yet. She has gone to the bank, but she hasn't taken the mail to the post office yet. She also hasn't written her monthly report. She has already met with the personnel officer about her maternity leave, but she hasn't spoken to the boss yet about her salary. She has sent a fax to the company's office in Tokyo. She hasn't read the office manager's memo about recycling. And she hasn't seen the training video about the new computer system. Allison is probably going to stay late at the office today so she can do all the things she hasn't done yet.

 READING *CHECK-UP*

Q & A

Allison's co-workers are asking her about the things she has done today. Using this model, create dialogs based on the story.

A. Allison, have you _____ yet?

B. { Yes, I have. }
{ No, I haven't. }

LISTENING

Carl is going to have a party at his apartment this Saturday night. This is the list of things that Carl needs to do to get ready for the party. Check the things on the list that Carl has already done.

- ___ go to the supermarket
- ___ clean the apartment
- ___ get balloons at the party store
- ___ buy some new dance music
- ___ hang up the decorations
- ___ make the food
- ___ tell the neighbors about the party
- ___ give the dog a bath

They've Been Dancing for Ten Hours

(I have)	I've
(We have)	We've
(You have)	You've
(They have)	They've
(He has)	He's
(She has)	She's
(It has)	It's

} been working.

A. How long have your friends been dancing?

B. They've been dancing for ten hours.

---

1. *wait for the bus*
since 8 o'clock

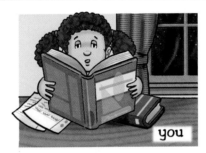

2. *study*
for five hours

3. *work here*
for thirty-five years

4. *argue*
since we got here

5. *go out*
for three months

6. *leak*
since last week

7. *live in Florida*
since they retired

8. *snore*
all night

9.

What Have They Been Doing?

(I have)	I've	
(We have)	We've	
(You have)	You've	
(They have)	They've	written.
(He has)	He's	
(She has)	She's	
(It has)	It's	

(I have)	I've	
(We have)	We've	
(You have)	You've	
(They have)	They've	been writing.
(He has)	He's	
(She has)	She's	
(It has)	It's	

A. Cynthia looks tired. What has she been doing?

B. She's been taking orders.

A. How many orders has she taken?

B. She's taken more than one hundred.

A. Wow! That's a lot of orders!

B. That's right. She's never taken that many orders before.

1. *give tennis lessons
   more than 20*

2. *write memos
   more than 25*

3. *assemble cell phones
   at least 75*

4. *draw portraits*
around 30

5. *read resumes*
more than 200

6. *deliver packages*
over 50

7. *sing songs*
at least 40

8. *sell tee shirts*
well over 300

9. *do sit-ups*
at least 90

10. *see patients*
around 45

11. *build sandcastles*
10 or 11

12. *make smoothies*
more than 150

How to Say It!

Expressing Surprise

Wow! — That's incredible!

Gee! — That's amazing!

Boy! — That's unbelievable!

You're kidding! — I can't believe it!

Practice the conversations in this lesson again. Express surprise in different ways.

INTERVIEW *How Long Have You ... ? / How Long Did You ... ?*

Interview another student. Then tell the class about the student you interviewed.

Where do you live now?
How long have you lived there?
Where did you live before?
How long did you live there?

Where do you (work/go to school) now?
How long have you (worked/gone to school) there?
Where did you (work/go to school) before?
How long did you (work/go to school) there?

They Had Done That Before

the day before

I
He
She
It } had eaten.
We
You
They

A. Did Andrew eat lunch at Burger Town yesterday?

B. No. He didn't want to. He had eaten lunch at Burger Town the day before.

the weekend before

1. Did Sheila drive to the beach last weekend?

the night before

2. Did you go dancing last night?

the morning before

3. Did Paul make pancakes for breakfast yesterday morning?

the day before

4. Did your children have peanut butter and jelly sandwiches for lunch yesterday?

the evening before

5. Did you and your friends see a movie yesterday evening?

the Saturday before

6. Did the Browns take their children to the aquarium last Saturday afternoon?

It Had Already Begun

A. Did Alan get to the movie on time?

B. No, he didn't. By the time he got to the movie, it had already begun.

1. *plane*
take off

2. *bank*
close

3. *play*
start

4. *game*
begin

5. *meeting*
end

6. *train*
leave the station

7. *ferry*
sail away

8. *space launch*
happen

9. *graduation ceremony*
finish

11

They Had Been Going Out for a Long Time

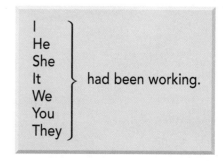

| I |
| He |
| She |
| It | had been working.
| We |
| You |
| They |

A. Is it true that Dave and his girlfriend broke up?

B. Yes, it is.

A. I'm sorry to hear that. How long had they been going out?

B. They had been going out for a long time.

Is it true that . . .

1. you had to cancel your trip to Hawaii?
plan it

2. your husband got laid off at the factory?
work there

3. your grandparents had to sell their house?
live there

4. your daughter injured herself and couldn't participate in the gymnastics competition?
train for it

5. your son got sick and couldn't perform in the school play?
rehearse for it

6. you came down with the flu and you couldn't take the SAT test?
prepare for it

IT WASN'T THE WEDDING THEY HAD PLANNED

Albert and Helen Porter had worked very hard to prepare for their daughter Ashley's wedding last July. Ashley had always wanted to get married at home in an outdoor ceremony. Albert and Helen had spent months planning the wedding and getting their house ready for the celebration.

On the night before the wedding, as Albert and Helen went to sleep, they felt totally prepared for this special day. They had repainted the house. They had planted new flowers and bushes in the yard. They had even taken down the rusty old swing set that Ashley had played on as a child. They had rented a tent and a dance floor. They had set up tables and chairs. And they had hung decorations all around the yard.

However, when Albert and Helen woke up early on the morning of the wedding, they couldn't believe what had happened. There had been a big thunderstorm during the night. The tent had fallen down. The tables and chairs had tipped over. And all the decorations had blown away. And it was still raining!

Albert and Helen, not to mention Ashley, were extremely upset. But they quickly decided to move the celebration indoors. It wasn't the wedding they had planned, but it was still a wonderful day, and all their family and friends had a great time.

✔ READING *CHECK-UP*

TRUE, FALSE, OR MAYBE?

Answer True, False, or Maybe (if the answer isn't in the story.)

1. Ashley got married last spring.
2. She didn't want to get married indoors.
3. Ashley doesn't have any brothers or sisters.
4. The night before the wedding, Albert and Helen felt they had done everything to prepare for the wedding.
5. It had stopped raining by the time Albert and Helen woke up.

Sometimes we work hard to prepare for something—a test, a performance, a party, a special event, or something else. Sometimes things go well, and sometimes they don't. Write in your journal about something you had worked hard to prepare for. What was it? How long had you prepared for it? How had you prepared? What happened?

PRONUNCIATION   Reduced *have, has,* & *had*

Listen. Then say it.

How long have you been married?

How long has he owned this car?

How long had he been rehearsing for it?

Say it. Then listen.

How long have we been waiting?

How long has she been sick?

How long had they been living there?

CHAPTER SUMMARY

GRAMMAR

PRESENT PERFECT TENSE

(I have)	I've	
(We have)	We've	
(You have)	You've	
(They have)	They've	eaten.
(He has)	He's	
(She has)	She's	
(It has)	It's	

I		
We	haven't	
You		
They		eaten.
He		
She	hasn't	
It		

Have	I we you they	eaten?
Has	he she it	

Yes,	I we you they	have.
	he she it	has.

No,	I we you they	haven't.
	he she it	hasn't.

PRESENT PERFECT CONTINUOUS TENSE

(I have)	I've	
(We have)	We've	
(You have)	You've	
(They have)	They've	been working.
(He has)	He's	
(She has)	She's	
(It has)	It's	

PAST PERFECT TENSE

I He She It We You They	had eaten.

PAST PERFECT CONTINUOUS TENSE

I He She It We You They	had been eating.

KEY VOCABULARY

IRREGULAR VERBS

be – was/were – been	eat – ate – eaten	grow – grew – grown	sing – sang – sung
begin – began – begun	fall – fell – fallen	know – knew – known	speak – spoke – spoken
blow – blew – blown	fly – flew – flown	ride – rode – ridden	swim – swam – swum
do – did – done	get – got – gotten	run – ran – run	take – took – taken
draw – drew – drawn	give – gave – given	see – saw – seen	wear – wore – worn
drive – drove – driven	go – went – gone	set – set – set	write – wrote – written

Perfect Modals:
Should Have
Might Have
May Have

Could Have
Must Have

- **Evaluating People's Activities**
- **Job Interviews**
- **Expressing Possibility**
- **Making Deductions**

- **Expressing Concern About Others**
- **Apologizing**
- **Recounting Difficult Situations**

VOCABULARY PREVIEW

1. answer the phone
2. apologize
3. daydream
4. fail
5. get lost
6. get stuck in *traffic*
7. hand over
8. oversleep
9. refuse
10. shake hands
11. skip *dessert*
12. yell

He Should Have Spoken Louder

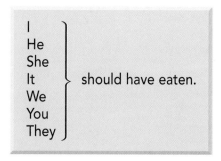

I	
He	
She	
It	should have eaten.
We	
You	
They	

A. Did Richard speak loud enough at the meeting this morning?

B. No, he didn't. He **should have spoken** louder.

---

1. Did Gail run fast enough during the marathon?

   faster

2. Did Fred drive carefully enough during his driving test?

   more carefully

3. Did Mr. and Mrs. Lopez get to the airport early enough?

   earlier

4. Did you and your classmates study hard enough for the science quiz?

   harder

5. Did Jason write legibly enough on his employment application?

   more legibly

6. Did you take the cookies out of the oven soon enough?

   sooner

7. Did Sally speak confidently enough at her job interview?

   more confidently

8. Did Brian dance well enough at the audition?

   better

She Shouldn't Have Driven to Work Today

Alice

I
He
She
It
We
You
They
} shouldn't have eaten.

A. Why is Alice upset?

B. She thinks she **shouldn't have driven** to work today. She **should have taken** the train.

Carl

1. *buy a typewriter*
   get a computer

Donna

2. *take Advanced French last semester*
   take Beginning French

you

3. *cook vegetable stew for my guests*
   make a salad

you and your wife

4. *see a movie last night*
   stay home and watch TV

Michael

5. *wear jeans to a job interview today*
   wear a suit

Mr. and Mrs. Parker

6. *go on a safari for their vacation*
   go to the beach

Jennifer

7. *write her composition on the bus*
   do it at home

Eric

8. *eat an entire cake for dessert*
   have just one piece

THEY DIDN'T DO AS WELL AS THEY SHOULD HAVE

Barry didn't do as well as he should have at a job interview today. He didn't get the job, and he now realizes that he should have done a few things differently. He should have spoken more confidently, he should have told more about his previous experience, and he probably should have worn more conservative clothes.

In addition, he shouldn't have arrived late for his appointment. He shouldn't have asked questions only about vacations and sick days. And he DEFINITELY shouldn't have eaten his lunch in the interviewer's office. Barry will certainly do a few things differently the next time he has a job interview!

Vicky didn't do as well as she should have in a tennis tournament yesterday. She didn't win, and she now realizes that she should have done a few things differently. She should have practiced more during the week, she should have done more warm-up exercises before the tournament, and she probably should have gotten a good night's sleep the night before.

Furthermore, she shouldn't have used her old tennis racket. She shouldn't have eaten such a large breakfast that morning. And she DEFINITELY shouldn't have gone out dancing with her friends the night before. Vicky will certainly do a few things differently the next time she plays in a tennis tournament!

✔ READING CHECK-UP

TRUE, FALSE, OR MAYBE?

Answer True, False, or Maybe (if the answer isn't in the story).

1. Barry didn't speak confidently about himself at the interview.
2. He didn't get the job because he didn't have previous experience.
3. Barry likes to go on vacations and gets sick very often.
4. Vicky didn't get a good night's sleep the night before the tournament.
5. She used her old tennis racket during the tournament.
6. Vicky goes out dancing with her friends very often.

How About You?

Tell about a time when you didn't do as well as you should have. What was the situation? What should you have done differently?

LISTENING

Listen and choose the best answer based on the conversation you hear.

1. a. They should have gotten to the party earlier.
   b. They should have left later.

2. a. He should have spoken more softly.
   b. He shouldn't have spoken softly.

3. a. He should have dressed more comfortably.
   b. He should have spoken more confidently.

4. a. He should have studied harder.
   b. He should have written more legibly.

5. a. He shouldn't have left them in the oven.
   b. He shouldn't have taken them out of the oven.

6. a. She should have gotten a good night's sleep last night.
   b. She should have gotten up earlier this morning.

IN YOUR OWN WORDS

FOR WRITING AND DISCUSSION

What should you do if you want to do well at a job interview?

What should you talk about?
What should you ask about?
What should you wear?
What should you take with you?
When should you arrive?

(In your answers, use "You should . . .")*

* "You should" = "a person should."

She Might Have Gone to the Bank

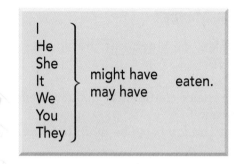

| I
He
She
It
We
You
They | might have
may have | eaten. |

A. I wonder why Sheila hasn't come back from lunch yet.

B. I'm not sure. She { **might have** / **may have** } **gone** to the bank.

A. Hmm. Maybe you're right.

I wonder why . . .

1. Bob was late for the meeting
get stuck in traffic

2. Professor Jones didn't come to class yesterday
be sick

3. Mr. and Mrs. Lane didn't come to our party
forget about it

4. Jimmy was late for school this morning
miss the bus

5. Peggy didn't want to go to the play with us
see it already

6. the neighbors haven't returned our ladder
break it

7. Dad left the rock concert early
have a headache

8. Grandma and Grandpa aren't answering their phone
go away for the weekend

READING

GEORGE HASN'T COME TO ENGLISH CLASS

George hasn't come to English class this evening, and all the students in the class are wondering why.

Henry thinks he might have gotten sick. Linda thinks he might have had a doctor's appointment. Mr. and Mrs. Kim think that one of George's children may have caught a bad cold. Carla thinks he may have had to work overtime. Mr. and Mrs. Sato think he might have gone to the airport to meet his relatives who are arriving from overseas. And Maria thinks he may have decided to study in another school.

All the students are curious about why George hasn't come to English class this evening . . . and they're a little concerned.

COMPLETE THE STORY

Complete this story about your English teacher. In your story, use names of students in your class.

Our English teacher hasn't come to class today, and all the students are wondering why.

_____ thinks _____.

_____ thinks _____.

_____.

_____.

_____.

And I think _____.

We're all curious about why our English teacher hasn't come to class today . . . and we're a little concerned.

21

He Could Have Gotten Lost!

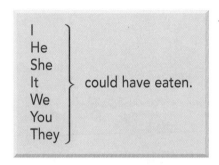

I	
He	
She	
It	could have eaten.
We	
You	
They	

A. If you ask me, Jack shouldn't have gone hiking by himself in the mountains.

B. You're right. He **could have gotten lost**!

1. *swim to the other side of the lake*
   drown

2. *play baseball in the rain*
   catch a bad cold

3. *ride her bicycle downtown during rush hour*
   get hurt

4. *move his piano by himself*
   break his back

5. *use her computer during a thunderstorm*
   be electrocuted

6. *go skating on the town pond*
   fall through the ice

7. *shovel all the snow in the driveway*
   have a heart attack

8. *argue with a police officer*
   wind* up in jail

9.

* wind – wound – wound

22

He Must Have Overslept

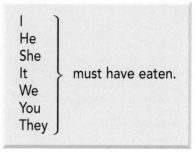

| I He She It We You They | } must have eaten. |

A. Richard came to work late today.

B. I'm really surprised to hear that. He NEVER comes to work late!

A. I know. He **must have overslept**.

B. You're probably right.

---

1. Maria missed English class all last week.
be very sick

2. Gary skipped dessert at the restaurant today.
go on a diet

3. Mrs. Grimsley smiled at her employees this morning.
be in a very good mood

4. Peter handed in his homework late this morning.
have a problem with his computer

5. Beverly yelled at me this morning.
be very upset

6. Walter was in a terrible mood today.
"get up on the wrong side of the bed"

7. You talked in your sleep last night.
have a bad dream

8. Rover refused to eat his dinner.
eat too many dog biscuits during the day

I'm a Little Concerned

I
He
She
It
We
You
They

must have
might have   eaten.
may have

A. Timmy looks frightened! He **must have seen a scary movie** today.

B. I'm not so sure. He {MIGHT **have** / MAY **have**} **seen a scary movie**, but that doesn't usually make him so frightened.

A. I'm a little concerned. Maybe we should talk to him.

B. That's a good idea.

A. Janet looks tired! She **must have worked overtime** today.

B. I'm not so sure. She {MIGHT **have** / MAY **have**} **worked overtime**, but that doesn't usually make her so tired.

A. I'm a little concerned. Maybe we should talk to her.

B. That's a good idea.

1. Mr. Jenkins looks exhausted!
swim fifty laps

2. Rachel looks upset!
fail an exam

3. Steve looks angry!
have a fight with his landlord

4. Margaret looks tired!
jog for a long time

5. Wayne looks upset!
have an argument with the boss

6. Our English teacher looks disappointed!
find a lot of mistakes in our homework

7. Rick looks exhausted!
do a lot of sit-ups

8. Senator Wilson looks tired!
shake* a lot of hands

* shake – shook – shaken

I Want to Apologize to You

A. I want to apologize to you.

B. What for?

A. You must have been very angry with me yesterday.

B. I don't understand. Why should I have been angry with you?

A. Don't you remember? We had planned to **see a movie** yesterday, but I completely forgot!

B. Don't worry about it. Actually, I owe YOU an apology.

A. You do? Why?

B. I couldn't have **seen a movie** with you anyway. I had to **take care of my little sister** yesterday . . . and I completely forgot to tell you.

A. That's okay. Maybe we can **see a movie** some other time.

A. I want to apologize to you.

B. What for?

A. You must have been very angry with me yesterday.

B. I don't understand. Why should I have been angry with you?

A. Don't you remember? We had planned to _go to the beach_ yesterday, but I completely forgot!

B. Don't worry about it. Actually, I owe YOU an apology.

A. You do? Why?

B. I couldn't have _gone to the beach_ with you anyway. I had to _study for my final exams._ yesterday . . . and I completely forgot to tell you.

A. That's okay. Maybe we can _go to the beach_ some other time.

1. *go to the beach*
   study for my final exams

2. *have lunch*
   go to an important meeting

3. *take a walk in the park*
   visit a friend in the hospital

4.

How to Say It!

Apologizing

I want to apologize to you.   I need to apologize to you.   I owe you an apology.   I apologize.   I'm sorry.

Practice the conversations in this lesson again. Use different expressions for apologizing.

LUCKY PEOPLE

Gary must have been daydreaming while he was driving to work yesterday. He drove through a red light at the busiest intersection in town. Fortunately, he didn't hit anyone. Gary was lucky. He could have caused a terrible accident.

Mrs. Chen must have been very scared yesterday. There was a big, mean dog outside while she was putting out the garbage. Fortunately, the dog didn't see her. Mrs. Chen was lucky. That big, mean dog might have bitten her.

Howard must have been extremely irritable this morning. He was rude to his supervisor when she pointed out a mistake he had made. Fortunately, his supervisor was in a good mood, and she didn't get angry. Howard was lucky. His supervisor could have fired him.

Ms. Kendall must have been feeling very brave last night. She refused to hand over her purse to a man who was trying to mug her. Fortunately, the man got scared and ran away. Ms. Kendall was very lucky. She might have gotten hurt.

Mr. and Mrs. Gray must have had a lot of financial problems last year. They were never able to pay their rent on time. Fortunately, their landlord was very understanding. Mr. and Mrs. Gray are pretty lucky. Their landlord could have evicted them.

Irwin must have been very lonely yesterday. All evening he made long-distance phone calls to his friends throughout the country. Fortunately, most of his friends weren't home. Irwin was very lucky. He could have run up quite a big phone bill.

✔ READING CHECK-UP

TRUE, FALSE, OR MAYBE?

Answer True, False, or Maybe (if the answer isn't in the story).

1. Gary wasn't paying attention while he was driving to work. *T*
2. Gary caused a terrible accident. *F*
3. Mrs. Chen doesn't like dogs. *M*
4. The dog didn't bite Mrs. Chen. *T*
5. Howard was in a good mood yesterday. *M*
6. Howard's supervisor is rarely in a bad mood. *T*
7. Ms. Kendall didn't give her purse to the man. *T*
8. Ms. Kendall had a lot of money in her purse. *M*
9. Mr. and Mrs. Gray couldn't pay their rent on time last year. *T*
10. The landlord evicted Mr. and Mrs. Gray. *F T*
11. Irwin's friends live throughout the country. *T*
12. Irwin never communicates with his friends by e-mail. *M*

WHICH WORD IS CORRECT?

1. Mr. and Mrs. Johnson didn't get to the train station on time. They (should have   **must have •**) left their house earlier.
2. Alan was late for work today. He (**should have•**   must have) overslept.
3. You're very lucky. You (**could have•**   must have) gotten hurt.
4. I (may have   **couldn't have•**) gone skiing with you anyway. I had to work.
5. Susan was an hour late for the meeting this morning. She (**might have•**   should have) gotten stuck in traffic.
6. Arnold's cake tasted terrible! He (**may have •**   should have) taken it out of the oven sooner.
7. I shouldn't have taken chemistry. I definitely (**must have•**   should have) taken biology.
8. Janet wasn't paying attention. She (**must have•**   should have) been daydreaming.
9. My cousin Ronald (shouldn't have   **couldn't have•**) swum to the other side of the lake. He (**must have**   could have) drowned!
10. Roberta didn't come to the company picnic last Saturday. She (should have   **may have•**) forgotten about it.

How About You?

| Tell about a time when something bad *could have* happened to you, but didn't. What was the situation? What could have happened? | Tell about a time when you were
. . . lonely.
. . . scared.
. . . irritable.
. . . brave. |

PRONUNCIATION Reduced *have*

Listen. Then say it.

He should have spoken louder.

She might have been sick.

They may have gone away.

Say it. Then listen.

You could have gotten hurt.

I must have overslept.

We shouldn't have gone there.

Write in your journal about a time when you did something and then you thought later that you should have done it differently. What did you do? What do you think you should have done?

CHAPTER SUMMARY

GRAMMAR

PERFECT MODALS:

SHOULD HAVE

I He She It We You They	**should have** eaten.

SHOULDN'T HAVE

I He She It We You They	**shouldn't have** eaten.

MUST HAVE

I He She It We You They	**must have** been upset.

MIGHT HAVE/MAY HAVE

I He She It We You They	**might have may have**	eaten.

COULD HAVE

I He She It We You They	**could have** gotten lost.

KEY VOCABULARY

ACTIONS

answer the phone
daydream
fail
get lost
get stuck in *traffic*

hand over
refuse
shake hands
skip *dessert*
yell

ADVERBS

arrive **late**
dance **well**
do things **differently**
dress **comfortably**
drive **carefully**
get to ___ **early**
practice **more**

run **fast**
speak **confidently**
speak **loud**
speak **softly**
study **hard**
take ___ out **soon**
write **legibly**

ADJECTIVES

advanced
beginning
brave
concerned
curious
entire
exhausted

financial
irritable
lonely
scared
understanding
unimportant

Passive Voice
Relative Pronouns

- Discussing Creative Works
- Describing Tasks Accomplished
- Discussing Things That Have Happened to People
- Describing Accomplishments

- Securing Services
- Automobile Repairs
- Historical Narratives
- Discussing Opinions

VOCABULARY PREVIEW

1. bicyclist
2. casserole
3. courier
4. decorations
5. dinosaur skeleton

6. flowerpot
7. identification card
8. invention
9. mural
10. pickpocket

11. poodle
12. puddle
13. sidewalk
14. uniform
15. windowsill

This Is a Very Scary Short Story!

Edgar Allan Poe wrote this short story.
This short story **was written** by Edgar Allan Poe.

A. This is a very scary short story!

B. I think so, too.

A. Who wrote it?

B. I'm not sure. I think it **was written** by Edgar Allan Poe.

A. This is a very elegant uniform!

B. I think so, too.

A. Who wore it?

B. I'm not sure. I think it **was worn** by Napoleon.

1. This is a very old airplane!
fly • the Wright Brothers

2. This is a beautiful sonata!
compose • Mozart

3. This is really a fascinating movie!
direct • *Fellini*

5. This is a very interesting invention!
invent • *Thomas Edison*

7. This is an amazing dinosaur skeleton!
find • *archeologists in Asia*

found   fond

9. This is a very good photograph of you!
take • *Uncle George*

Took   Taken

11. This is an extremely colorful mural!
do • *the students at Central High School*

did   done.

4. This is a very funny political cartoon!
draw • *Richard Hill*

drew   drawn!

6. This is a magnificent portrait!
paint • *Rembrandt*

8. This is an impressive building!
design • *Frank Lloyd Wright*

10. This is a very sad poem!
write • *Shakespeare*

wrote   writing!

12. This is a delicious tuna casserole!
make • *Millie Swensen*

made   made

It's Already Been Written

Somebody has written the report.
The report **has been written**.

Somebody has hung up the decorations.
The decorations **have been hung up**.

A. Do you want me to write the accident report?

B. No. Don't worry about it. It's already **been written**.

A. Do you want me to hang up the decorations?

B. No. Don't worry about it. They've already **been hung up**.

1. *sweep the floor*

2. *do the dishes*

swept

done

3. *set the alarm* set

4. *set up the meeting room*

5. *give out the paychecks* given

6. *distribute the mail*

7. *make the beds in Room 219* made .

8. *hide the teacher's birthday present* hidden

9. *take out the trash* taken

10. *send the packages* sent

11. *feed the monkeys*

12. *sing the National Anthem*

Have You Heard About . . . ?

A. Have you heard about Helen?

B. No, I haven't. What happened?

A. She **was given** a raise last week.

B. That's great! That's the second time she's **been given** a raise this year!

A. Have you heard about Henry?

B. No, I haven't. What happened?

A. He **was hurt** during a football game last week.

B. That's terrible! That's the second time he's **been hurt** during a football game this year!

1. *Maria promoted*

2. *our mail carrier bitten by a dog*

3. *Aunt Martha invited to the White House*

4. *Stuart*
   hit by a car

5. *Mr. and Mrs. Tyler*
   robbed

6. *Jennifer*
   offered a movie contract

7. *Frank*
   fired

8. *Mrs. Mendoza*
   taken to the hospital

9. *Arthur*
   rejected by the army

10. *Diane*
    sent to Honolulu on
    business

11. *Albert*
    chosen "Employee of the
    Month"

12.

How to Say It!

Reacting to Good News

That's great!
That's fantastic!
That's wonderful!
That's great news!
That's fantastic news!
That's wonderful news!
I'm happy to hear that!
I'm glad to hear that!

Reacting to Bad News

That's terrible!
That's awful!   *horrible*
That's a shame!   *vergüenza*
That's a pity!   *compasión*
That's too bad!
What a shame!
What a pity!
How awful!
I'm sorry to hear that!

Practice the conversations in this lesson again. React to good and bad news in different ways.

ALAN ALMOST DIDN'T GET TO WORK THIS MORNING

Alan almost didn't get to work this morning. As he was leaving his apartment building, he was hit on the head by a flowerpot that had just fallen from a windowsill. As he was walking to the bus stop, he was bitten by a dog, stung* by a bee, and splashed by a car that had just driven through a puddle. And while he was waiting for the bus, he was almost run over by a bicyclist who was riding on the sidewalk.

While he was riding on the bus, his wallet was stolen by a pickpocket who was standing behind him. All his money and identification cards were taken. As he was walking into his office building, he was accidentally knocked down by the courier who delivers the overnight mail. And when Alan finally arrived at work an hour late, he was yelled at by a manager who was in a very bad mood.

Poor Alan! What a way to begin the day!

* sting–stung–stung

 ## READING *CHECK-UP*

TRUE, FALSE, OR MAYBE?

Answer True, False, or Maybe (if the answer isn't in the story).

1. As Alan was leaving his apartment building, he was hit on the head by a windowsill.
2. As he was walking to the bus stop, a dog bit him, a bee stung him, and a car splashed him.
3. A bicyclist almost hit Alan.
4. Alan had a lot of money in his wallet.
5. Alan accidentally knocked down the courier who delivers the overnight mail.
6. Alan was yelled at because he wasn't on time for work.

How About You?

Have you ever had a bad day when everything went wrong? When? How did you feel? What happened?

READING

A VERY EXCITING YEAR

In January Amelia was hired as a secretary by the Inter-Tel Company, which makes international telephone equipment. In March she was sent to school by the company to study statistics and information technology. In April she was given a raise. Just two months later, she was promoted to the position of supervisor of her department.

In August she was chosen "Employee of the Month," which is a great honor at Inter-Tel. In October she was given another raise. In November she was invited to apply for a position in the company's overseas office in Bangkok. And in December she was given the new job and was flown to Thailand to begin work.

Amelia certainly has had a very exciting year. She can't believe all the wonderful things that have happened to her since she was hired just twelve months ago.

✔ READING CHECK-UP

CHOOSE

1. The interviewer liked Amelia's resume, so she was given the _____.
   a. raise
   b. position

2. After Amelia had worked at the company for five months, she was _____.
   a. promoted
   b. hired

3. In August Amelia was _____ "Employee of the Month."
   a. chosen
   b. given

4. In December she was sent overseas _____ her company.
   a. as
   b. by

5. Over one hundred people had _____ the position in Bangkok.
   a. been invited to
   b. applied for

6. Many wonderful things have happened to Amelia since she was _____ twelve months ago.
   a. hired
   b. fired

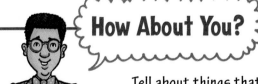

How About You?

Tell about things that have happened to you during the past twelve months.

It's Being Repaired Right Now

Somebody is repairing my computer.
My computer is **being repaired**.

A. Hello. Is this Carol's Computer Repair Shop?

B. Yes, it is. Can I help you?

A. Yes, please. This is Mr. Lopez. I'm calling about my computer. Has it **been repaired** yet?

B. Not yet. It's **being repaired** right now.

A. I see. Tell me, when can I pick it up?

B. It'll be ready in about an hour.

A. Thank you.

A. Hello. Is this _____?

B. Yes, it is. Can I help you?

A. Yes, please. This is _____. I'm calling about my _____. (Has it/Have they) been _____ yet?

B. Not yet. (It's/They're) being _____ right now.

A. I see. Tell me, when can I pick (it/them) up?

B. (It'll/They'll) be ready in about an hour.

A. Thank you.

1. *Ms. Evans*
   VCR • fix

2. *Ted Clark*
   pants • take in

3. *Mrs. Withers*
   will • rewrite

4. *Glen Burns*
   poodle • clip

5. *Jennifer Wu*
   wedding cake • make

6.

READING

JOE'S AUTO REPAIR SHOP

Wilma Jones has been having a lot of trouble with her car recently, so she decided to take it to Joe's Auto Repair Shop to be fixed. The car is being repaired there right now, and it is receiving a LOT of attention from Joe and the other mechanics at his shop.

The engine is being tuned up. The oil is being changed. The battery is being charged. The brakes are being adjusted. The front bumper is being repaired. The broken headlight is being replaced. The hood is being repainted. The tires are being checked. And the broken rear window is being fixed.

Wilma is aware that she'll probably be charged a lot of money for these repairs. But she's confident that her car will be returned to her in excellent condition by the fine people who work at Joe's Auto Repair Shop.

✔ READING *CHECK-UP*

Q & A

Wilma Jones is calling Joe's Auto Repair Shop to find out about her car. Using this model, make questions and answers based on the story.

A. Have you *tuned up the engine* yet?
B. *It's* being *tuned up* right now.

LISTENING

Listen and choose the best line to continue the conversation.

1. a. Do you want me to send them?
   b. Who sent them?

2. a. Do you want me to make them?
   b. Who made them?

3. a. Was your cat hurt badly?
   b. Was your dog hurt badly?

4. a. Is she going to go?
   b. Is he going to go?

5. a. When will Mrs. Green begin working?
   b. When will Mr. Fleming begin working?

6. a. When will Mrs. Davis start her new job?
   b. When will Ms. Clark start her new job?

7. a. Oh, good. I'll pick it up in an hour.
   b. Oh, good. Call me when it's been fixed.

8. a. Oh, good. I'll pick it up right now.
   b. Oh, good. I'll pick it up when it's ready.

TALK ABOUT IT! *What's Your Opinion?*

> Answers **should be written** in your notebook.
> Students **should be required** to take an examination.
> Camping **shouldn't be allowed** in public parks.

Talk about these issues with other students.

1. Should your native language be spoken during English class?

2. Should students be allowed to use dictionaries in class?

3. Should high school students be required to do community service?

4. Should young men and women be required to serve in the armed forces?

5. Should animals be used for medical research?

6. Should skateboarding be permitted on city streets and sidewalks?

7. Should camping be permitted in public parks?

8. Should children be allowed to see any movies they want to?

43

A NATIONAL HISTORIC LANDMARK

This building, which is the original headquarters of the Lord and Lady Department Store Company, was designed by the famous architect Archibald Morgan. It was built by the Vanderpool Construction Company. Construction was begun in 1845 and was completed in 1847. The building was officially opened in ceremonies that were held on April 13, 1847. These ceremonies were attended by the mayors of several cities, the governor, and the vice president of the United States.

The building's interior was destroyed by a fire that broke out in the early hours of the morning of February 3, 1895. After the fire, the building wasn't used for several years.

During World War I the structure was used as a warehouse for clothing and other materials that were sent to our soldiers overseas. After the war, the interior was rebuilt. Electric lights and modern plumbing were installed, and the Lord and Lady Department Store was officially reopened on June 17, 1921.

Since its opening day, the Lord and Lady Department Store has been considered one of the finest examples of nineteenth-century American architecture. The store has been visited by the presidents and prime ministers of many countries.

On December 5, 1973, this building was officially registered as a U.S. National Historic Landmark.

✔ READING *CHECK-UP*

WHAT'S THE ANSWER?

1. Who was the building designed by?
2. Who was the building built by?
3. When was construction begun?
4. When was it completed?
5. When was the building officially opened?
6. Who were the opening ceremonies attended by?
7. What happened on February 3, 1895?
8. What was the building used for during World War I?
9. When was the interior rebuilt?
10. When was the building reopened?
11. Since its opening day, what has the building been considered?
12. What happened on December 5, 1973?

CHOOSE

1. Cable TV service was _____ in my apartment this afternoon.
   a. opened
   b. installed

2. Our high school prom was _____ by all the students in our class.
   a. attended
   b. visited

3. The factory downtown was _____ by the fire.
   a. rebuilt
   b. destroyed

4. The construction has been completed, and now the store can be _____.
   a. rebuilt
   b. reopened

5. Our City Hall is _____ by many tourists because it's a very historic building.
   a. visited
   b. registered

6. Their wedding ceremony wasn't _____ outside because it rained.
   a. considered
   b. held

IN YOUR OWN WORDS

FOR WRITING AND DISCUSSION

Tell a story about the history of the place where you were born or a place where you have lived. You might want to use some of the following words in your story:

attacked	discovered
begun	founded
built	invaded
captured	liberated
closed	opened
conquered	rebuilt
destroyed	settled

Listen. Then say it.

The engine is being tuned.

The brakes are being adjusted.

The store has been rebuilt.

Say it. Then listen.

The oil is being changed.

The tires are being checked.

The construction has been completed.

Write in your journal about students' rights and responsibilities in your school. What are students required to do? What are they allowed to do? What are they not allowed to do?

CHAPTER SUMMARY

GRAMMAR

PASSIVE VOICE

This short story **was written** by Edgar Allan Poe.
The decorations **have been hung up**.
My computer **is being repaired**.

Students **should be required** to take an examination.
Camping **shouldn't be allowed** in public parks.

RELATIVE PRONOUNS

He was hit by a flowerpot **that** had just fallen.
He was knocked down by the courier **who** delivers the overnight mail.

She was hired by the Inter-Tel company, **which** makes international telephone equipment.

KEY VOCABULARY

NOUNS

accident report	mayor
architect	meeting room
architecture	mural
bicyclist	opening day
casserole	overnight mail
ceremonies	pickpocket
construction	plumbing
courier	political cartoon
decorations	poodle
dinosaur skeleton	puddle
electric lights	short story
example	sidewalk
flowerpot	soldiers
governor	sonata
headquarters	statistics
identification card	structure
information technology	uniform
interior	warehouse
invention	will
materials	windowsill

AUTOMOBILE

battery
brakes
bumper
engine
headlight
hood
oil
rear window
tires

ADJECTIVES

amazing
colorful
fascinating
finest
impressive
magnificent
original
overseas
scary

VERBS

adjust	promote
break out	rebuild
charge	register
check	reject
clip	reopen
complete	repaint
design	replace
destroy	rewrite
hold	splash
install	sting
knock down	tune up
offer	

SIDE by SIDE Gazette

Volume 4   Number 1

Inventions That Changed the World

Famous Inventions and Their Inventors

The first known antibiotic, penicillin, was discovered by Alexander Fleming in 1928. It was made from a mold called *penicillin*, which could kill bacteria. Since then, many other antibiotics have been discovered. Millions of lives have been saved by these antibiotics.

X-rays were discovered in 1895 by a German professor, Wilhelm Roentgen. People all over the world were amazed by his invention, the X-ray machine. This invention was so important that Roentgen was awarded the first Nobel Prize for Physics in 1901.

The screw was created over 2000 years ago. It was invented by a Greek named Archimedes. It was first used for watering fields. A person turned the giant wooden screw, which pulled water from lakes or rivers and sent it into fields. The water was used for irrigating crops. Much later, in the 1600s, screws were made by carpenters to hold things together. Today the screw is mass-produced and has an unlimited number of uses.

The telephone was invented by Alexander Graham Bell, a doctor and speech teacher for the deaf. The first phone call was made by Bell in 1876. He had spilled acid on his pants and wanted his assistant, Thomas Watson, to help him. The first words spoken on the telephone were "Mr. Watson, come here! I need you!"

Television was invented in 1926 by John Logie Baird, a Scottish inventor. Baird's television certainly didn't look like a television today! It was made out of a box, knitting needles, a cake tin, a bicycle lamp, and a cardboard disc. Electronic televisions like the ones we have today were invented by Vladimir Zworykin in the 1920s in the United States.

The first computer was built in 1946 by two American engineers, J. Presper Eckert, Jr., and John W. Mauchly. It was developed for the army, and it was so large that it took up an entire room! Later, in 1971, the "microchip" was invented, and small home computers were first produced for personal use. Today computers are involved in almost everything we do and are found almost everywhere we go.

FACT FILE

Time Line of Major Inventions

- **3500 B.C.:** the wheel invented
- **3000 B.C.:** toothpaste first used by Ancient Egyptians
- **2000 B.C.:** the sundial first used for telling time
- **1000 B.C.:** kites first flown in China
- **200 B.C.:** the screw invented in Greece for irrigation
- **105:** the first paper created by the Chinese
- **1200:** the abacus, a counting machine, introduced in China
- **1440:** the first printing press set up in Germany
- **1590:** the microscope invented
- **1791:** the first bicycle ridden in France
- **1876:** the telephone invented by Alexander Graham Bell
- **1895:** X-rays discovered by Wilhelm Roentgen
- **1903:** the first airplane flight made by Orville and Wilbur Wright
- **1908:** the first gas-powered cars assembled in the United States
- **1926:** the first television built by John Logie Baird in Scotland
- **1926:** penicillin discovered by Alexander Fleming
- **1946:** the world's first computer turned on
- **1961:** the first manned space flight launched by the Soviet Union
- **1977:** the first cell phones constructed by Bell Laboratory in New Jersey
- **1982:** compact discs introduced by Sony and Philips Corporations
- **1991:** the World Wide Web established

The wheel was invented about 3500 B.C. The first bicycle was ridden in France in 1791. When was the first microscope invented? What happened in 1876? Talk with other students about these major inventions.

Ancient and Modern Wonders of the World

The Pyramids were built as tombs for the kings of ancient Egypt more than 5000 years ago. They were constructed without machines and with very few tools. The kings were buried with many jewels, furniture, and personal treasures.

The Colosseum in Rome, Italy, was completed in 80 A.D. It was built as an amphitheater, a place for people to go to be entertained. Fights between gladiators, fights with beasts such as lions and tigers, and other battles were held there.

Machu Picchu was built high in the Andes Mountains of Peru by Incas during the period 1460 to 1470 A.D. Experts believe it was constructed for religious purposes. It was abandoned in the 1500s, but no one knows why.

Stonehenge is a group of huge stones that were erected in England during the period 2800 to 1800 B.C. No one knows who it was built by or why. Some people think it was used as a sundial to follow the position of the sun. Others think it might have been built as a temple for worshipping the sun.

The Taj Mahal in India was constructed by order of Shah Jahan in the 17th century. It was designed as a tomb for his favorite wife, who had died giving birth to their child. It was built by 20,000 men from many different countries. It is considered one of the most beautiful tombs in the world.

The Temple of Angkor Wat in Cambodia is one of the largest religious structures in the world. It was constructed in the 12th century and took about 30 years to build. The temple was dedicated to the Hindu god Vishnu. Today the site is being repaired and preserved by the United Nations and many countries.

The Great Wall of China was begun in the 3rd century B.C., and it wasn't completed until hundreds of years later. The wall was rebuilt, strengthened, and enlarged in the centuries that followed. It is estimated to be about 6000 kilometers in length. It is said that the Great Wall is even visible from the moon!

Tenochtitlan, an elaborate city in Mexico, was established in 1325 A.D. It was built on an island in the middle of a lake. According to legend, the Aztecs were told by an omen, or sign, to construct the city there. It was inhabited by 200,000 to 300,000 people. Mexico City is located on its ruins.

The Panama Canal was constructed in Panama to connect the Atlantic and Pacific Oceans. In 1901, the United States was given permission to build the canal. It was opened on August 15, 1914. The canal is used by more than 9000 ships a year, and it is maintained by approximately 8000 workers.

Which of these wonders would you like to visit? Why? What are some other wonders of the ancient or modern world that you know about?

Interview

A *Side by Side Gazette* reporter recently interviewed international photojournalist *Sam Turner. Sam has been taking news photographs for twenty years. His photos have been published in newspapers and magazines all over the world.*

Q: Sam, can you tell us a little about yourself?

A: Sure. Both my parents are American, but I was born in Sydney, Australia. My parents both worked for a big American bank, and they were transferred to Australia just before I was born. My parents and I spent a lot of time exploring Australia during our vacations. I was very influenced by those trips. I was really inspired by the natural beauty of the country.

Q: How did you first become interested in photography?

A: I was given a camera for my tenth birthday, and I took it along on a family trip to the Australian Outback. When I showed my photos to people, they were really impressed! I was encouraged to study photography.

Q: So did you go to photography school?

A: Yes, and I was chosen by my teachers as one of the most promising students in the school. One of my photos was selected for a national photo competition, and it won an award.

Q: What has been the most memorable event in your life?

A: I was invited by a group of mountain climbers to travel with them to Mt. Everest and take their photographs at the base camp at the bottom of the mountain. They were wonderful people, and it was a beautiful place.

Q: What photo have you been dreaming about taking someday?

A: I'd like to take a photo from the TOP of Mt. Everest! I'm not physically prepared for that right now, but someday I hope to make that journey. It's my dream!

FUN with IDIOMS

Do You Know These Expressions?

_____ **1.** I was given the ax at work today.

_____ **2.** Everybody was told about it, but I was left in the dark.

_____ **3.** I was held up in traffic.

_____ **4.** I was blown away by the mechanic's repair bill.

a. I was surprised.

b. I was stuck.

c. I was fired.

d. I didn't know.

Dear Side by Side,

We are students in Ms. Baxter's class at the English Language School, and we have a question about the passive voice. It's very confusing for us. It requires different verb forms and different word order in the sentences. Why do we need it?

Sincerely,

"Actively Against the Passive"

Dear "Actively Against the Passive,"

Many students are confused by the passive voice. It is used very commonly in English, especially in written language such as textbooks and newspaper and magazine articles. The passive voice is often used when it isn't known or it isn't important who performs the action. For example:

The wheel was invented in 3500 B.C.
The school was built in 1975.
The paychecks have been given out.
The computer is being repaired.

When it is known or it is important who performs an action, the passive voice is sometimes used and is followed by a phrase that begins with the word "by." For example:

The telephone was invented by Alexander Graham Bell.
This novel was written by Alice Walker.

The passive voice is also used to focus attention on the subject of the passive sentence. For example:

The building was opened in 1847.
It was destroyed by a fire in 1895.
It was reopened in 1921.

So, even if you don't use the passive voice very much when you speak English, you will see it often in print, and you will also hear it being used. As time goes on, we're sure you'll feel more comfortable with the passive voice. Thanks for writing!

Sincerely,

Side by Side

Global Exchange

Kate1: Hi. Sorry I haven't been in touch recently. It's been a very busy time. I have some incredible news! Last month I was chosen "Outstanding Student of the Year" at my school. I was invited to a special ceremony at our city hall. During the ceremony, I was given a beautiful plaque to hang on my wall, and I was offered a college scholarship. The ceremony was attended by the mayor and lots of other important people in our city. My parents and my grandparents were there, and they were very proud. How have you been? What's new?

MarcJ: Hi. It's great to hear from you again. It's been a while. Congratulations on your award. I also have some news, but it isn't good news like yours. Two weeks ago I was hurt badly during a soccer game. I was taken to the hospital in an ambulance. The X-rays showed that my leg was broken in two places, so it was put in a cast. According to my doctor, I won't be allowed to play soccer for the rest of the season. As you can imagine, I'm very disappointed, but I'm confident I'll be back on the team next year. G2G* Talk to you soon.

Send a message to a keypal. Tell about some good or bad things that have happened to you recently.
*G2G = Got to go.

LISTENING   NEWS REPORT

"News Report" True or False?

____ ❶ **a.** A van was hit by a bicyclist.

____ ❷ **b.** Joe Murphy lost the race for mayor.

____ ❸ **c.** Five people were injured in the fire.

____ ❹ **d.** The Terriers defeated the Eagles.

____ ❺ **e.** The police discovered the robbery.

What Are They Saying?

Embedded Questions

- Asking for Information
- Indicating Uncertainty
- Referring People to Someone Else
- Reporting a Crime
- Reporting a Missing Person

VOCABULARY PREVIEW

1. conductor
2. flight attendant
3. librarian
4. lifeguard
5. prime minister
6. real estate agent
7. receptionist
8. security guard
9. ticket agent
10. usher
11. birthmark
12. plane ticket
13. restrooms
14. scar
15. tonsils

I Don't Know Where the Cheese Is

Where is the bank?	I don't know where the bank is.
What is he doing?	I don't know what he's doing.
Why were they crying?	I don't know why they were crying.
When can he visit us?	I don't know when he can visit us.

A. Where is the cheese?

B. I don't know where the cheese is.

1. Where are the plane tickets?

2. What was his license number?

3. What are they arguing about?

4. When will the bus from Chicago arrive?

5. Who was the third prime minister of Canada?

6. How long have the Wilsons been married?

7. How long has Alice been working here?

8. Who should I vote for?

9. When is Santa Claus going to come?

Practice the conversations on this page again. Use these expressions instead of "I don't know."

I don't remember . . .	I'm not sure . . .
I can't remember . . .	I have no idea . . .
I've forgotten . . .	

I Don't Know When the Movie Begins

Where does he live?	I don't know where he lives.
How often do they come here?	I don't know how often they come here.
How did she break her leg?	I don't know how she broke her leg.

A. When does the movie begin?

B. I don't know when the movie begins.

1. Where does Mr. Webster work?

2. How much do eggs cost this week?

3. Why did Richard get fired?

4. What time did the plane to Miami leave?

5. How often does the ice cream truck come by?

6. Where did Mom and Dad get married?

7. What does this word mean?

8. What did we do in class yesterday?

9. Why do young people like such loud music?

Practice the conversations on this page again. Use these expressions instead of "I don't know."

I don't remember . . .   I'm not sure . . .
I can't remember . . .   I have no idea . . .
I've forgotten . . .

Do You Know What the Homework Assignment Is?

Where is the park?	Do you know where the park is?
When does the train leave?	Do you know when the train leaves?

A. Do you know what the homework assignment is?

B. I'm sorry. I don't know. You should ask Ronald.
HE can tell you what the homework assignment is.

A. Do you know how much this computer costs?

B. I'm sorry. I don't know. You should talk to that salesperson.
SHE can tell you how much this computer costs.

1. *ask that security guard*

2. *check with the ticket agent*

3. *ask Grandpa*

4. *talk to the boss*

5. *check with the mechanic*

6. *ask your sister*

7. *ask the people next door*

8. *talk with his supervisor*

9. *ask your nurse*

10.

How to Say It!

Asking for Information

Do you know
Can you tell me
Could you tell me
Could you please tell me
Could you possibly tell me
Do you have any idea
Do you by any chance know

} *what the homework assignment is?*

Practice the conversations in this lesson again. Ask for information in different ways.

ROSEMARY SMITH WAS ROBBED

Rosemary Smith was robbed about an hour ago while she was walking home from work. She's at the police station now, and she's having some trouble giving information to the police.

She knows that a man robbed her about an hour ago, but she simply can't remember any of the details. She doesn't know how tall the man was. She isn't sure how heavy he was. She can't remember what color hair he had. She has no idea what color eyes he had. She doesn't remember what he was wearing. She has forgotten what kind of car he was driving. She can't remember what color the car was. She has no idea what the license number was. And she doesn't even know how much money was taken!

Poor Rosemary! The police want to help her, but she can't remember any of the details.

✓ READING *CHECK-UP*

Q & A

You're the police officer. You're trying to get information from Rosemary Smith about the robbery. Using this model, make questions and answers based on the story.

A. Can you tell me* *how tall the man was*?
B. I'm sorry. I don't know *how tall he was*.

> *Or: Do you know . . . ?   Do you have any idea . . . ?
>   Could you tell me . . . ?   Do you by any chance know . . . ?

CHOOSE

1. I'm not sure _____.
   a. where do they live
   b. where they live

2. She doesn't know _____.
   a. when the store opens
   b. when does the store open

3. Do you remember _____?
   a. where you put the car keys
   b. where did you put the car keys

4. Could you tell me _____?
   a. why is the boss angry
   b. why the boss is angry

5. I have no idea _____.
   a. how much they spent
   b. how much did they spend

6. He's forgotten _____.
   a. what is her name
   b. what her name is

READING

A "SURPRISE" QUIZ

Mrs. Murphy is giving her students a "surprise" history quiz today, and Jeffrey isn't very happy about it. He has been absent for the past several days, and he's having a lot of trouble answering the questions.

He doesn't know who the nineteenth president of the United States was. He isn't sure when the Civil War ended. He doesn't remember when California became a state. He has forgotten where George Washington was born. He can't remember how many people signed the Declaration of Independence. He doesn't know where Abraham Lincoln was assassinated. He has forgotten why Washington, D.C. was chosen as the capital. And he has no idea what Alexander Graham Bell invented!

Jeffrey is very upset. He's sure he's going to fail Mrs. Murphy's "surprise" history quiz.

✔ READING CHECK-UP

Q & A

The history quiz is over, and Mrs. Murphy is going over the answers with her students. Using the story as a guide, complete the following conversation.

A. Who knows who the nineteenth president of the United States was?
B. I do. It was Rutherford B. Hayes.
A. And who can tell me _____?
C. I can. It ended in 1865.
A. Does anyone know _____?
D. Yes. It became a state in 1850.
A. Who remembers _____?
E. I remember. He was born in Virginia.
A. Can anybody tell me _____?
F. Yes. It was signed by 56 people.
A. Who knows _____?
G. He was assassinated at Ford's Theater in Washington, D.C.
A. And who can tell me _____?
H. It was chosen because the northern and southern states agreed it was a good location for the capital.
A. And finally, who remembers _____?
I. I do. He invented the telephone.
A. Very good, class!

Do You Know If Surfing Is Allowed at This Beach?

Is Tom in school today?

Do you know { if / whether } Tom is in school today?

I don't know { if / whether } Tom is in school today.

Does Mary work here?

Do you know { if / whether } Mary works here?

I don't know { if / whether } Mary works here.

Is surfing allowed at this beach?

A. Do you know { if / whether } surfing is allowed at this beach?

B. I'm not really sure. Why don't you ask the lifeguard?

SHE can tell you { if / whether } surfing is allowed at this beach.

Did anybody here find a cell phone?

A. Do you know { if / whether } anybody here found a cell phone?

B. I'm not really sure. Why don't you ask the cashier?

HE can tell you { if / whether } anybody here found a cell phone.

1. *Do you by any chance know . . . ?*
   ask Mr. Blake

2. *Could you please tell me . . . ?*
   ask the bus driver

3. *Can you tell me . . . ?*
   check with the librarian

4. *Do you know . . . ?*
   speak with Dr. Bell

5. *Do you by any chance know . . . ?*
   talk to our supervisor

6. *Do you have any idea . . . ?*
   ask the usher

7. *Do you know . . . ?*
   speak to the flight attendant

8. *Do you by any chance know . . . ?*
   check with the conductor

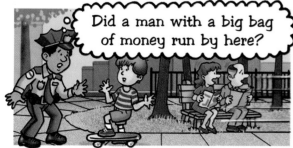

9. *Can you tell me . . . ?*
   ask those people over there

10.

READING

AT THE MIDTOWN MEDICAL CLINIC

It's a busy afternoon at the Midtown Medical Clinic. Lots of people are sitting in the waiting room and thinking about the questions they're going to ask the doctor.

Frank wants to know if he broke his arm. Mrs. Wilkins needs to know if she has lost too much weight. Arnold wants to find out whether he should go on a diet. Mrs. Parker is wondering whether her children have the measles. Dan is hoping to find out if he'll be able to play in the soccer match next week. Linda is going to ask the doctor whether she has to have her tonsils taken out. Edward expects to find out whether he needs glasses. And Vicki is anxious to know if she's pregnant.

Everybody is waiting patiently, but they hope they don't have to wait too long. They're all anxious to hear the answers to their questions.

 READING *CHECK-UP*

Q & A

The people in the story are registering with the receptionist at the Midtown Medical Clinic. Using this model, create dialogs based on the story.

A. I'd like to see the doctor, please.
B. What seems to be the problem?
A. I'm wondering (if/whether) *I broke my arm.*
B. All right. Please take a seat in the waiting room. The doctor will see you shortly.

CHOOSE

1. Do you know if ____?
   a. is it going to rain
   b. it's going to rain

2. I'm not really sure whether ____.
   a. the bus will be late
   b. will the bus be late

3. The teacher can tell us ____.
   a. if we'll have a test
   b. whether will we have a test

4. Can you tell me ____?
   a. whether have they moved
   b. whether they have moved

5. I'm anxious to know ____.
   a. how did I do on the exam
   b. how I did on the exam

6. Jackie is wondering ____.
   a. whether she got the job
   b. did she get the job

LISTENING

Listen and decide where the conversation is taking place.

1. a. a book store   b. a library
2. a. a kitchen   b. a supermarket
3. a. a laundromat   b. a department store
4. a. a concert hall   b. a museum

5. a. an airport   b. an airplane
6. a. a school   b. a doctor's office
7. a. a clinic   b. a hospital
8. a. a bus station   b. a bus stop

INTERACTIONS

Practice with another student. Read about each situation. Brainstorm more questions. Then create a conversation, using the following expressions:

Do you know . . . ?	Could you please tell me . . . ?	Do you by any chance know . . . ?
Can you tell me . . . ?	Could you possibly tell me . . . ?	I'd like to know . . . .
Could you tell me . . . ?	Do you have any idea . . . ?	I'm wondering . . . .

Melinda wants to buy a house. She's visiting a house right now and talking with a real estate agent.

How old is this house?
Does the roof leak?

_____ ?
_____ ?
_____ ?

Do you know how old this house is?
Can you tell me if the roof leaks?

_____
_____
_____

Michael is planning to go to college next year. He's visiting a college right now and talking with a person in the admissions office.

What courses do students
   have to take?
Does the school have a good
   library?

_____ ?
_____ ?
_____ ?

Could you please tell me what courses
   students have to take?
I'd like to know whether the school has
   a good library.

_____
_____
_____

ROLE PLAY *I Want to Report a Missing Person*

Police Department
Missing Person Information Sheet

1. What is your name?

2. What is the missing person's name?

3. What is his/her address?

4. How old is he/she?

5. How tall is he/she?

6. How much does he/she weigh?

7. Does this person have any scars, birthmarks, or other special characteristics?

8. Where was he/she the last time you saw him/her?

9. What was he/she wearing at that time?

10. What was he/she doing?

11. What is your relationship to the missing person?

12. What is your telephone number?

13. When can we reach you at that number?

A student in your class is missing! Call the police!

I want to report a missing person!

1.

Please tell me what your name is.

2.

And can you tell me what the missing person's name is?

3. Can you tell me ...?

4. Do you know ...?

5. Can you tell me ...?

6. Do you have any idea ...?

7. Do you by any chance know ...?

8. Can you tell me ...?

9. Could you possibly tell me ...?

10. And can you tell me ...?

11. Could you please tell me ...?

12. Please tell me ....

13. Can you tell me ...?

PRONUNCIATION Reduced *you*

Listen. Then say it.

Do you know where the bank is?

Do you have any idea how much this costs?

Can you tell me if the train will arrive on time?

Say it. Then listen.

Do you know if I have the flu?

Do you have any idea if we're almost there?

Can you tell me whose dog this is?

SIDE *by* **SIDE JOURNAL**

Some people wonder a lot about the future. They wonder where they will live. They wonder what they will do. They wonder if they will be happy. What do **you** wonder about? What questions do you ask yourself about the future? Write about it in your journal.

CHAPTER SUMMARY

GRAMMAR

EMBEDDED QUESTIONS:

WH-QUESTIONS WITH BE

Where is the bank?
Do you know where the bank is?
I don't know where the bank is.

What is he doing?
Do you know what he's doing?
I don't know what he's doing.

Why were they crying?
Do you know why they were crying?
I don't know why they were crying.

WH-QUESTIONS WITH DO/DOES/DID

Where does he live?
Do you know where he lives?
I don't know where he lives.

How often do they come here?
Do you know how often they come here?
I don't know how often they come here.

How did she break her leg?
Do you know how she broke her leg?
I don't know how she broke her leg.

YES/NO QUESTIONS

Is Tom in school today?
Do you know { if / whether } Tom is in school today?
I don't know { if / whether } Tom is in school today.

Does Mary work here?
Do you know { if / whether } Mary works here?
I don't know { if / whether } Mary works here.

KEY VOCABULARY

OCCUPATIONS

conductor
flight attendant
librarian
lifeguard
prime minister

real estate agent
receptionist
security guard
ticket agent
usher

NOUNS

birthmark
capital
details
information sheet
missing person

plane ticket
restrooms
scar
surprise quiz
tonsils

VERBS

assassinate
check with
come by
mean

rob
sign
vote

Conditional:
Present Real (If _____ Will)
Present Unreal (If _____ Would)
Hope-Clauses

- Describing Plans and Intentions
- Consequences of Actions
- Discussing Future Events
- Expressing Hopes
- Asking for and Giving Reasons
- Making Deductions
- Emergencies

VOCABULARY PREVIEW

1. coin
2. pollution
3. report card
4. representative
5. wishing well
6. drop in
7. encourage
8. hold hands
9. increase
10. sneeze
11. aggressive
12. burnt
13. carsick
14. dressed up
15. missing

They Aren't Sure

if _____ will _____

A. How is Angela going to get to work tomorrow?

B. She isn't sure.
If the weather is good, she'll probably ride her bicycle.
If the weather is bad, she'll probably take the bus.

---

1. What's Ben going to do this Saturday?

If it's sunny, ____.
If it rains, ____.

2. What are you going to do tomorrow?

If I still have a cold, ____.
If I feel better, ____.

3. What are Mr. and Mrs. Taylor going to do tonight?

If they're tired, ____.
If they feel energetic, ____.

4. Where is Roy going to have lunch today?

If he's busy, ____.
If he isn't busy, ____.

5. Where is Lisa going to go after school today?

If she has a lot of homework, ____.
If she doesn't have a lot of homework, ____.

6. What's Alan going to have for dessert this evening?

If he decides to stay on his diet, ____.
If he decides to forget about his diet, ____.

Do You Think . . . ?

if _____ might _____

A. Do you think Rover should come to the beach with us today?

B. No, I don't. If he comes to the beach with us today, he might get carsick.

---

1. Do you think Abigail should go to school today?

give her cold to the other children

3. Do you think Roger should quit his job?

have trouble finding another one

5. Do you think we should try to break up that fight?

get hurt

7. Do you think I should marry Norman?

regret it for the rest of your life

2. Do you think I should skip my history class today?

miss something important

4. Do you think I should put some more salt in the soup?

spoil it

6. Do you think Ricky should stay up and watch TV with us?

have trouble getting up in the morning

8.

I Hope Our Team Wins the Game Tomorrow

I hope it rains tomorrow.
I hope it doesn't rain tomorrow.

A. I hope our team wins the game tomorrow.

B. I hope so, too.

A. I hope the teacher doesn't give a quiz today.

B. I hope not, too.

1.

2.

3.

4.

5.

6.

7.

8.

I Hope

A. Do you think the train will be crowded?

B. I hope not.
If the train is crowded, we'll have to stand.
And if we have to stand, we'll be exhausted by the time we get to work!

A. You're right. I hope the train isn't crowded.

1.

A. Do you think the boss will retire this year?

B. I hope not.
If _____, his son will take his place.
And if _____, everybody will quit!

A. You're right. I hope _____.

2.

A. Do you think the economy will get worse this year?

B. I hope not.
If _____, I'll have to get a second job.
And if _____, my family will be very upset!

A. You're right. I hope _____.

3.

A. Do you think Mr. Mudge will increase our rent this year?

B. I hope not.
If _____, we won't be able to pay it.
And if _____, we'll have to move!

A. You're right. I hope _____.

4.

A. Do you think our computer will be at the repair shop for a long time?

B. I hope not.
If _____, we won't have access to the Internet.
And if _____, we won't be able to read our e-mail!

A. You're right. I hope _____.

THE WISHING WELL

There's a park in the center of Danville, and in the park there's a wishing well. It's a very popular spot with the people of Danville. Every day people pass by the wishing well, drop in a coin, and make a wish. Some people make wishes about their jobs, others make wishes about the weather, and lots of people make wishes about their families and friends.

Today is a particularly busy day at the wishing well. Many people are coming by and making wishes about their hopes for the future.

Ralph hopes he sells a lot of used cars this month. If he sells a lot of used cars, he'll receive a large year-end bonus.

Patricia hopes she gets a raise soon. If she gets a raise, her family will be able to take a vacation.

Andy hopes it snows tomorrow. If it snows, his school might be closed.

Nancy and Paul hope they find a cheap apartment soon. If they find a cheap apartment, they won't have to live with Paul's parents anymore.

Claudia hopes her next movie is a big success. If it's a big success, she'll be rich and famous.

John hopes he gets good grades on his next report card. If he gets good grades, his parents will buy him the CD player he has wanted for a long time.

Mr. and Mrs. Clark hope they live to be a hundred. If they live to be a hundred, they'll be able to watch their grandchildren and great-grandchildren grow up.

J. P. Morgan hopes the nation's economy improves next year. If the economy improves, his company's profits will increase.

And Wendy hopes she gets accepted to medical school. If she gets accepted to medical school, she'll become a doctor, just like her mother and grandfather.

You can see why the wishing well is a very popular spot with the people of Danville. Day after day, people pass by, drop in their coins, and hope that their wishes come true.

✔ READING CHECK-UP

Q & A

You're talking with the people in the story. Using this model, create dialogs based on the story.

A. I hope *I sell a lot of used cars this month*.
B. Oh?
A. Yes. If *I sell a lot of used cars, I'll receive a large year-end bonus*.
B. Well, good luck! I hope *you sell a lot of used cars*!
A. Thanks.

CHOOSE

1. We hope our landlord doesn't ____ our rent.
   a. increase
   b. improve

2. Jennifer is very smart. She gets good ____ in all her subjects.
   a. cards
   b. grades

3. People go to the wishing well and make ____ about the future.
   a. profits
   b. wishes

4. Have you ____ today's mail yet?
   a. received
   b. accepted

5. Arthur hopes his new Broadway play is a big ____.
   a. access
   b. success

6. The company couldn't increase my salary this year, but they gave me a very nice ____.
   a. raise
   b. bonus

If They Lived Closer, They'd Visit Us More Often

(I would)	I**'d**
(He would)	He**'d**
(She would)	She**'d**
It would	
(We would)	We**'d**
(You would)	You**'d**
(They would)	They**'d**

work.

if _____ would _____

A. Why don't our grandchildren visit us more often?

B. They don't live close enough.
If they lived closer, they'd visit us more often.

A. Why isn't Alexander able to lift weights?

B. He isn't strong enough.
If he were* stronger, he'd be able to lift weights.

* If [I, he, she, it, we, you, they] were . . .

1. Why don't I feel energetic?
You don't sleep enough.
If _____.

2. Why isn't Sally a good driver?
She isn't careful enough.
If _____.

3. Why doesn't Brian get good grades?
   He doesn't study enough.
   If _____.

5. Why doesn't Amy have friends at school?
   She isn't outgoing enough.
   If _____.

7. Why aren't most Americans in good
   physical condition?
   They don't exercise enough.
   If _____.

9. Why doesn't my car get better gas
   mileage?
   You don't tune up your engine often enough.
   If _____.

11. Why don't our representatives in Congress
    do something about pollution?
    *They aren't concerned enough about the
    environment.*
    If _____.

4. Why aren't you satisfied with your job?
   I don't get paid enough.
   If _____.

6. Why doesn't Stan have a yearly checkup?
   He doesn't care enough about his health.
   If _____.

8. Why isn't Melvin a good salesman?
   He isn't aggressive enough.
   If _____.

10. Why don't you and Janet get along
    with each other?
    We don't have enough in common.
    If _____.

12. Why doesn't our English teacher buy a new
    pair of shoes?
    He doesn't make enough money.
    If _____.

If She Didn't Like Her Job, She Wouldn't Work So Hard

if _____ wouldn't (would not) _____

A. I wonder why Olivia works so hard.

B. She must like her job.

A. You're probably right.
If she didn't like her job, she wouldn't work so hard.

A. I wonder why Paul is so dressed up.

B. He must have a job interview.

A. You're probably right.
If he didn't have a job interview, he wouldn't be so dressed up.

1. I wonder why Gary is so nervous.
He must have an exam today.

2. I wonder why our supervisor is shouting at us today.
She must be in a bad mood.

3. I wonder why Rover is barking at the door.
He must want to go outside.

5. I wonder why Gregory makes so many mistakes.
He must be careless.

7. I wonder why Donald gets into so many fights.
He must like to argue with people.

9. I wonder why I'm sneezing so much.
You must be allergic to my perfume.

4. I wonder why Melanie wants to be a schoolteacher.
She must like children.

6. I wonder why Beth is home tonight.
She must have to take care of her little brother.

8. I wonder why my brother and his girlfriend hold hands all the time.
They must be in love.

10.

How to Say It!

Expressing Agreement

- You're probably right.
- I think you're right.
- I think that's right.
- I think that's true.
- That's probably true.

Practice the conversations in this lesson again. Express agreement in different ways.

READING

THEY WOULD BE WILLING TO IF . . .

For several months, Frederick has been pressuring his wife, Doris, to go to the dentist, but she refuses to go. The reason is that she can't stand the sound of the dentist's drill. Doris says that if the dentist's drill didn't bother her so much, she would be willing to go to the dentist. Frederick hopes his wife changes her mind and goes to the dentist soon.

For several months, Barry's family has been encouraging him to ask his boss for a raise, but Barry refuses to do it. The reason is that he's afraid his boss might get angry and say "No." Barry says that if he weren't afraid of his boss's reaction, he would be willing to ask for a raise. Barry's family hopes he changes his mind and asks for a raise soon.

✔ READING CHECK-UP

TRUE, FALSE, OR MAYBE?

Answer True, False, or Maybe (if the answer isn't in the story).

1. Frederick refuses to go to the dentist.
2. Doris is going to find a different dentist.
3. Doris would be willing to go to the dentist if the sound of the drill didn't bother her.
4. Barry isn't willing to ask for a raise right now.
5. If Barry asked for a raise, his boss would say "No."
6. Barry's family began to encourage him to ask for a raise one month ago.

LISTENING

Listen and choose the statement that is true based on what you hear.

1. a. It's raining today.
   b. It isn't raining today.

2. a. We have enough money.
   b. We don't have enough money.

3. a. Mrs. Carter isn't her English teacher.
   b. Mrs. Carter is her English teacher.

4. a. They might receive bonuses.
   b. The company's profits didn't increase.

5. a. He isn't allergic to trees.
   b. He isn't going hiking this weekend.

6. a. He isn't going to the movies tonight.
   b. He doesn't have to work tonight.

TALK ABOUT IT! Are You Prepared for Emergencies?

Talk with other students about these emergencies.

1. What would you do if you saw a bad accident?

2. What would you do if you saw someone having a heart attack?

3. What would you do if somebody in your family were missing?

4. What would you do if you were bitten by a dog?

5. What would you do if you were at the beach and you saw someone drowning?

6. What would you do if somebody came up to you on the street and tried to rob you?

7. What would you do if a fire broke out in your house or apartment?

8. What would you do if you were lying in bed and you heard someone trying to break into your house or apartment?

Think of some other emergencies and talk with other students about what you would do.

What would you do with the money if you won a million dollars on a TV game show? Write about it in your journal.

Listen. Then say it.

If I got paid more, I'd be satisfied with my job.

If she were more outgoing, she'd have friends at school.

Say it. Then listen.

If we had more in common, we'd get along better.

If you tuned up your car more often, it'd get better gas mileage.

CHAPTER SUMMARY

GRAMMAR

PRESENT REAL CONDITIONAL (IF___WILL)

If	I we you they	feel	better,	I'll we'll you'll they'll	eat dinner.
	he she it	feels		he'll she'll it'll	

PRESENT UNREAL CONDITIONAL (IF___WOULD)

If	I he she we you they	had more time,	I'd he'd she'd we'd you'd they'd	study more.

If	I he she we you they	didn't have an exam,	I he she we you they	**wouldn't** be nervous.

If	I he she we you they	were stronger,	I'd he'd she'd we'd you'd they'd	be able to do that.

If	I he she we you they	weren't careless,	I he she we you they	**wouldn't** make mistakes.

HOPE-CLAUSES

I We You They	hope	I we you they	get	a raise soon.
He She	hopes	he she	gets	

I hope it rains tomorrow.
I hope it doesn't rain tomorrow.

I hope the weather is nice this weekend.
I hope the weather isn't bad this weekend.

KEY VOCABULARY

VERBS

break up	get worse	miss
drop in	hold hands	skip
encourage	hope	sneeze
get accepted	increase	spoil
get paid	make a wish	

NOUNS

access	environment	representative
bonus	physical condition	sound
coin	pollution	spot
Congress	profits	success
drill	reaction	wish
economy	report card	wishing well

ADJECTIVES

aggressive
burnt
carsick
dressed up
important
missing

Feature Article
Fact File
Around the World
Interview
We've Got Mail!

SIDE by SIDE Gazette

Global Exchange
Listening
Fun with Idioms
What Are They
Saying?

Volume 4   Number 2

The Music of Wishes and Hopes

Songwriters often express wishes and hopes through their music. Their songs are filled with lyrics such as "If I could . . . ," "If I had . . . ," "If I were. . . ," I wish . . . ," and "I hope . . . ." Here are some favorite songs about wishes and hopes from the worlds of popular, folk, Broadway, country, and rock music.

"If I Had a Hammer": This famous folk song was originally written as a poem by Lee Hays, then put to music by Pete Seeger. The singer sings about what he would do to bring peace all over the land.
He sings that if he had a hammer, he'd hammer in the morning. If he had a bell, he'd ring it. If he had a song, he'd sing it. This popular tune was made famous by the folk singers Peter, Paul, and Mary.

"(If I Could Save) Time in a Bottle": In this song written by Jim Croce, the singer wishes he had more time to spend with his girlfriend. If it were possible, he would save time the way people save money. He would save the days in a bottle and then spend all the time with the one he loves.

"If I Had a Million Dollars": In this popular song sung by the Canadian group Barenaked Ladies, the leader of the group sings about what he would do if he had a million dollars. He would buy
the woman he loves a house, furniture, a car, an exotic pet, a green dress, and other things.

"I Hope You Dance": This song of hope is sung by the popular country music singer Lee Ann Womack. She sings about her hopes for the people she loves. She hopes they never go hungry or without love. She hopes they find joy in simple pleasures like the ocean. She hopes they appreciate what they have.

"If I Were a Bell": In this song from the musical *Guys and Dolls*, Sarah Brown sings about her feelings for the man she loves, a gambler named Sky Masterson. She is so happy that if she were a bell, she'd be ringing. If she were a gate, she'd be swinging.

"If I Were a Rich Man": In the musical *Fiddler on the Roof*, Tevye, a poor dairyman, sings that he wishes he were rich. If he were a rich man, he wouldn't have to work
hard, and he would build a big house for his family.

"(If I Could) Change the World": Singer Eric Clapton won a Grammy Award for this song from the movie *Phenomenon*. In this song, the singer wishes he could change the world and be with the girl he loves. If he could, he would be the center of her universe. He would be a king, and she would be a queen. But for now, he realizes it's impossible.

Try to find some of these songs and listen to them. Do you know other songs about wishes and hopes?

FACT FILE

Song Search

WORD	NUMBER OF SONGS WITH WORD IN TITLE
"if"	1130
"hope"	41
"wish"	149

Making Wishes

There are many different traditions and customs for making wishes around the world.

If you find a four-leaf clover, make a wish and then throw the clover away. (Ireland)

When you see a new moon, hold a coin up to the moon and wish for money. As the moon increases, your money will increase. (Jamaica)

If you make a wish as you throw a coin or a pebble into a wishing well, your wish may come true. (Many countries)

Make a wish before you blow out the candles on a birthday cake. (The United States and other countries)

If you open a nutshell and find two nuts instead of one, give one to a friend. Each of you should make a wish. If you're the person who remembers to say "lucky nut" the next morning, you will get your wish. (Russia)

At midnight on New Year's Eve, eat one grape for each of the twelve chimes of the clock. Make the same wish as you eat each grape and your wish will come true. (Spain, Portugal, and Venezuela)

If you catch a falling leaf, make a wish. (Japan)

When you see lightning, make a wish. (The Philippines)

Hold one end of a wishbone (from a chicken or turkey) while someone else holds the other end. Make a wish, then break the wishbone. If you get the longer piece, your wish will come true. (The United States)

When you see the first full moon of the year, make a wish. (Korea)

Stand with your back to a fountain. Throw three coins, one at a time, over your shoulder into the water. Each time make the same wish. If you hear the coins splash into the water three times, your wish will come true. (Europe)

When you see the first star in the evening sky, say this poem and make a wish:

Star light, star bright,
First star I see tonight.
I wish I may, I wish I might
Have the wish I wish tonight.

(Many countries with similar poems in different languages)

Which of these traditions for wishing did you know about? What are some traditions that you know?

Interview

A Side by Side Gazette
reporter asked these people:

Q: What would you do if you won a million dollars?

A: I don't know. I wouldn't quit my job, that's for sure! I wouldn't know what to do if I had so much free time.

A: I'd pay all my bills, and I'd pay off all my debts. I'd put the rest of the money in the bank.

A: I think I would quit my job and travel around the world.

A: I'd invest some money, and I'd save the rest for my children's college education.

A: I'd help my parents. They don't have a lot of money. I'd buy them a house in a nice neighborhood.

A: I'd give most of the money to charities that help people. I'd really feel good if I could do that.

A: All my life I've dreamed about starting my own business. I'd open up a flower shop, and my dream would come true.

FUN with IDIOMS

Do You Know These Expressions?

_____ 1. You're breaking my heart.

_____ 2. You light up my life.

_____ 3. You're a heel!

_____ 4. You've got me wrapped around your little finger.

a. I'm very happy.

b. I'll do anything for you.

c. I'm very sad.

d. You aren't a nice person.

We've Got Mail!

Dear Side by Side,

   I'm confused about the correct tense to use with the word "hope." It seems to me that the future tense should be used when someone expresses hope about the future. For example, I think a person should say, "I hope the weather will be nice tomorrow." But according to my teacher, the present tense should be used: "I hope the weather is nice tomorrow." And I'm sure I've heard English speakers use the future tense after the word "hope." Are these people making a grammar mistake?

                        Sincerely,
                        "Hoping for an Answer"

Dear "Hoping for an Answer,"

   Yes, those people are making a very common grammar mistake. We understand why you think the future tense should be used to express hope about the future. It seems to make sense. Unfortunately, grammar rules in English don't always make sense! In this case, the rule is that the present tense should be used. We hope this answers your question.

                        Sincerely,
                        Side by Side

Dear Side by Side,

   I have a question about the words "were" and "was" in conditional sentences. According to your book, the following sentences are correct:

   If he **were** stronger, he'd be able to lift weights.
   If I **were** bitten by a dog, I'd call the doctor.
   If she **weren't** in a bad mood, she wouldn't be shouting.
But I think it's better to use the word "was" instead of "were" in these sentences. Plus, I hear people use "was" in sentences like these all the time! Can you explain this?

                        Sincerely,
                        "Confused About Conditionals"

Dear "Confused About Conditionals,"

   Your question is wonderful because it shows the difference between grammatically correct English and the informal English people use every day. "Were" is the grammatically correct verb in these conditional sentences. However, it is indeed very common in informal speech for people to say "was." If you were a student in our classroom, we would encourage you to use "were." That's the correct form, and after all, you're studying the rules of the language!

                        Sincerely,
                        Side by Side

Send a message to a keypal. Tell about your plans for the weekend.

LISTENING

Tempo Airlines

Press

_e_ ①	**a.**	to plan a vacation
____ ②	**b.**	to repeat the menu
____ ③	**c.**	to fly in the U.S. or Canada
____ ④	**d.**	to speak to a representative
____ ⑤	**e.**	to find out about today's flights
____ ⑥	**f.**	to fly overseas
____ ⑦	**g.**	to get travel awards
____ ⑧	**h.**	to listen to airport check-in rules

What Are They Saying?

Present Unreal Conditional (continued)
Wish-Clauses

- Advice
- Expressing Wishes
- Job Satisfaction
- Expressing Ability
- Asking for and Giving Reasons
- Life in Cities and Suburbs

VOCABULARY PREVIEW

1. classified ad
2. day shift
3. night shift
4. full-time job
5. part-time job

6. baby food
7. baby picture
8. beard
9. driver's ed
10. fan

11. foreign language
12. obituary
13. pronunciation
14. taxes
15. voter

If I Were You

A. Do you think the boss would be angry if I went home early?

B. Yes, I do. I think she'd be VERY angry.

A. Do you really think so?

B. Yes. I'm positive. I wouldn't go home early if I were you.

A. I suppose you're right.

1. Do you think Ted would be disappointed if I missed his birthday party?

2. Do you think Mom would be angry if I drove her new car?

3. Do you think the neighbors would be annoyed if I practiced the drums now?

4. Do you think Mrs. Riley would be upset if I skipped English class tomorrow?

5. Do you think the owners of the building would be upset if I painted the kitchen purple?
Yes I do. If I were you I wouldn't

6. Do you think my parents would be disappointed if I dropped out of medical school?

7. Do you think Roy would be jealous if I went out with his girlfriend?

8. Do you think Dad would be mad if I borrowed his cell phone?

9. Do you think the voters would be upset if I raised taxes?

10. Do you think my fans would be unhappy if I got a haircut?

11. Do you think Matt would be embarrassed if I showed his baby pictures to his girlfriend?

12.

To Tell the Truth

A. I'm thinking of **growing a beard**. What do you think?

B. To tell the truth, I wouldn't **grow a beard** if I were you.

A. Why do you say that?

B. If you **grew a beard**, you'd probably **look very funny**.

A. Hmm. You might be right.

1. *buy a used car from Ralph Jones*
   spend a lot of money on repairs

2. *get a dog*
   be evicted from your apartment building

3. *start an Internet company*
   "lose your shirt"

4.

How to Say It!

Giving a Personal Opinion

To tell the truth,
To tell you the truth,
To be honest,   } *I wouldn't grow a beard.*
To be honest with you,
If you ask me,

Practice the conversations on this page again. Use different expressions for giving a personal opinion.

Wishes

Tom **lives** in Boston.   He **wishes** he **lived** in New York.

A. Do you enjoy driving a taxi?

B. Not really. I wish I drove a school bus.

A. Does Mr. Miller enjoy being a teacher?

B. Not really. He wishes he were an actor.

---

1. Does Alice enjoy living in the suburbs?
in the city

2. Does Barry enjoy being single?
married

3. Does Mrs. Dexter enjoy teaching music?
something else

4. Do you enjoy working the night shift?
the day shift

5. Does Vincent enjoy painting houses?
portraits

6. Does Ann enjoy having two part-time jobs?
one good full-time job

7. Do you enjoy being the vice president?
the president

8. Does Albert enjoy having a cat?
a dog

9.

"SICK AND TIRED"

Frank is "sick and tired" of selling used cars! He has been doing that for twenty-eight years. Frank wishes he sold something else. In fact, at this point in his life, he would be willing to sell ANYTHING as long as it wasn't used cars!

Peggy is "sick and tired" of writing classified ads and obituaries for the Midville Times! She has been doing that since 1989. Peggy wishes she wrote something else. In fact, at this point in her life, she'd be willing to write ANYTHING as long as it wasn't classified ads and obituaries!

Mr. Dellasandro is "sick and tired" of teaching driver's ed! He has been teaching that for the past twenty-one years. "Mr. D" wishes he taught something else. In fact, at this point in his life, he would be willing to teach ANYTHING as long as it wasn't driver's ed!

Patty and Jimmy are "sick and tired" of eating tuna fish sandwiches for lunch. They have been eating them for lunch every day for the past four years. Patty and Jimmy wish their parents would give them something else for lunch. In fact, at this point in their lives, they would be willing to eat ANYTHING for lunch as long as it wasn't tuna fish sandwiches!

✔ READING CHECK-UP

CHOOSE

1. Tom found his job through the _____.
   a. classified ads
   b. obituaries

2. If you don't visit Aunt Nellie in the hospital, she'll be very _____.
   a. disappointed
   b. sick and tired

3. I was _____ when my driver's ed teacher shouted at me in front of the other students.
   a. jealous
   b. embarrassed

4. I enjoy working the _____.
   a. night shift
   b. full time

5. Howard _____ the meeting because he had to go to the dentist.
   a. dropped out of
   b. skipped

6. This is a _____ of me that was painted when I was three years old.
   a. portrait
   b. photograph

They Wish They Could

A. Can Jeffrey cook?

B. No, he can't . . . but he wishes he could. If he could cook, he'd **invite his friends over for dinner**.

1. Can Brian dance?
go dancing every night

2. Can Cheryl type fast?
be able to leave work on time

3. Can Steve speak a foreign language?
be able to get a better job

4. Can Martha knit?
make sweaters for her grandchildren

5. Can Gary fix his car by himself?
save a lot of money

6. Can Mr. and Mrs. Bradley ski?
take their children skiing in Colorado

7. Can Abby play a musical instrument?
be able to march in the town parade

8. Can Jessica talk?
tell her parents she doesn't like her baby food

9. Can Richard roll his "Rs"?
have better pronunciation in Spanish

10.

Why Do You Say That?

| if _____ { could / would be able to } _____ |

A. You know, I wish my TV weren't fixed.

B. Why do you say that?

A. If it weren't fixed, { I could / I'd be able to } talk with my children.

A. You know, I wish my son didn't want to be a dentist.

B. Why do you say that?

A. If he didn't want to be a dentist, { I could / I'd be able to } convince him

to manage my shoe store when I retire.

1. *wear my new raincoat this Saturday*

2. *go to the beach*

3. *have a garden*

4. *see her more often*

5. *concentrate more on my work*

6. *go away for the weekend*

7. *invite my friends over to watch the Super Bowl*

8. *have some "peace and quiet" around the house*

READING

THEY WISH THEY LIVED IN THE CITY

The Anderson family lives in the suburbs, but they wish they lived in the city. If they lived in the city, Mr. Anderson wouldn't have to spend all his spare time mowing the lawn and working around the house. Mrs. Anderson wouldn't have to spend two hours commuting to work every day. Their son Michael would be able to take the bus to the baseball stadium. Their daughter, Jennifer, would be living close to all of her favorite book stores. And their other son, Steven, could visit the zoo more often. It would be very difficult for the Anderson family to move to the city now, but perhaps some day they'll be able to. They certainly hope so.

COMPLETE THE STORY

THEY WISH THEY LIVED IN THE SUBURBS

The Burton family lives in the city, but they _____ ¹ they lived in the suburbs. If they _____ ² in the suburbs, Mrs. Burton _____ ³ be able to plant a garden and grow vegetables. Mr. Burton _____ ⁴ have to listen to noisy city traffic all the time. Their son, Ken, _____ ⁵ have a backyard to play in. Their daughters, Betsy and Kathy, _____ ⁶ have to share a room. And their cat, Tiger, _____ ⁷ be able to go outside and play with the other cats. It _____ ⁸ be very difficult for the Burton family to move to the suburbs now, but perhaps some day they'll be _____ ⁹ to. They certainly hope so.

How About You?

Do you wish you lived someplace else? Where? Why?

Compare life in the city and life in the suburbs. What are the advantages and disadvantages of each?

READING

"ALL THUMBS"

Ethel can never fix anything around the house. In fact, everybody tells her she's "all thumbs." She wishes she were more mechanically inclined. If she were more mechanically inclined, she would be able to repair things around the house by herself.

Robert can't dance very well. In fact, all the girls he goes out with tell him he has "two left feet." Robert wishes he could dance better. If he could dance better, he wouldn't feel so self-conscious when he goes dancing.

Maria is having a hard time learning English. She's having a lot of trouble with English grammar and pronunciation. Maria wishes she had a "better ear" for languages. If she had a "better ear" for languages, she probably wouldn't be having so much trouble in her English class.

 ## READING *CHECK-UP*

MATCHING: *Do You Know These Expressions?*

____ 1. He's *all thumbs.*

____ 2. She's *handy* around the house.

____ 3. He has *a green thumb.*

____ 4. He's *all heart.*

____ 5. He's very *nosey.*

____ 6. She's got *a lot on her shoulders.*

____ 7. She always *keeps her chin up.*

____ 8. He's *up in arms.*

a. very kind

b. doesn't know how to fix things

c. optimistic

d. knows how to fix things

e. has many responsibilities

f. good at gardening

g. very angry

h. asks about other people

How About You?

Are you "all thumbs"? Do you have "two left feet"? Everybody has a few things he or she would like to do better. What do you wish you could do better? Why?

LISTENING

Listen and choose the statement that is true based on what you hear.

1. a. He has a dog.
   b. He doesn't have a dog.

2. a. She works the night shift.
   b. She works the day shift.

3. a. She's a musician.
   b. She's a teacher.

4. a. He doesn't have to take biology.
   b. He has to take biology.

5. a. She can't type fast.
   b. She can type fast.

6. a. They don't have a car.
   b. They don't live in the city.

PRONUNCIATION Reduced *would*

Listen. Then say it.

Do you think the boss would be angry?

Do you think the neighbors would be annoyed?

Do you think Roy would be jealous?

Do you think Ted would be disappointed?

Say it. Then listen.

Do you think my parents would be disappointed?

Do you think the voters would be upset?

Do you think Julie would be mad?

Do you think Matt would be embarrassed?

Write in your journal about something in your life you wish for. What do you wish? How would your life be different if your wish came true?

CHAPTER SUMMARY

GRAMMAR

PRESENT UNREAL CONDITIONAL (IF___WOULD)

Do you think the boss **would** be angry **if** I went home early?
I **wouldn't** go home early **if** I were you.

If	I he she we you they	could dance,	I'd he'd she'd we'd you'd they'd	go dancing.

If my TV weren't fixed,	I **could** I'd **be able to**	talk with my children.

WISH-CLAUSES

I We You They	wish	I we you they	lived in New York. were more athletic. could dance. didn't live here. weren't sick.
He She	wishes	he she	

KEY VOCABULARY

NOUNS

baby food
baby picture
beard
classified ad
day shift
driver's ed
fan
foreign language
full-time job
high-rise building

Internet company
night shift
obituary
part-time job
pronunciation
repairs
spare time
suburbs
taxes
view
voter

VERBS

borrow
commute
concentrate
convince
drop out of
evict
go out with
miss
raise
roll
show
skip

FEELINGS AND EMOTIONS

angry
annoyed
disappointed
embarrassed
jealous
mad
self-conscious
unhappy
upset

EXPRESSIONS

all thumbs
better ear
lose your shirt
peace and quiet
sick and tired
two left feet

7

Past Unreal Conditional (If _____ Would Have)
Wish-Clauses (continued)

- Asking for and Giving Reasons
- Making Deductions
- Discussing Unexpected Events
- Expressing Wishes and Hopes
- Consequences of Actions
- Rumors

VOCABULARY PREVIEW

1. audience
2. cactus plant
3. chemistry set
4. flu shot
5. income tax form
6. ingredients
7. metal detector
8. minister
9. mortgage
10. performance
11. postcard
12. printer
13. snowman
14. traffic light
15. wedding dress

If She Had Known . . .

if _____ would have _____

| I
He
She
It
We
You
They | would have eaten. |

A. Why didn't Brenda take her umbrella to work today?

B. She didn't know it was going to rain.
If she had known it was going to rain, she would have taken her umbrella to work today.

A. Why weren't you in class yesterday?

B. I wasn't feeling well.
If I had been feeling well, I would have been in class yesterday.

1. Why didn't Jason stop at the traffic light?
He didn't notice it.
If _he had notice it._ _He would have stopped._

2. Why didn't you go to the movies last night?
I wasn't in the mood to see a film.
If _I had been in the mood_ _I would have gone to see a film._

3. Why wasn't Mark on time for work today?
His alarm clock didn't ring.
If ——————————————.

4. Why didn't you hand in your paper today?
My printer wasn't working last night.
If ——————————————.

5. Why didn't the Kramers buy the house on Pine Street?
Their mortgage wasn't approved.
If ——————————————.

6. Why didn't Mr. and Mrs. Park enjoy their ski vacation?
There wasn't enough snow.
If ——————————————.

7. Why didn't you send us a postcard?
We didn't remember your address.
If ——————————————.

8. Why didn't you go to the party last night?
I wasn't invited.
If ——————————————.

9. Why didn't Mr. and Mrs. Sanchez enjoy the play last night?
They didn't have good seats.
If ——————————————.

10. Why wasn't Senator Harrington re-elected?
The people didn't trust him.
If ——————————————.

11. Why didn't Mr. Kelly's students give him a birthday present?
He didn't tell them it was his birthday.
If ——————————————.

12. Why wasn't Sophia asked to sing an encore last night?
The audience wasn't pleased with her performance.
If ——————————————.

I Wonder Why

A. I wonder why Charles ran by without saying hello.

B. He must have been in a hurry.

A. You're probably right. If he hadn't been in a hurry, he wouldn't have run by without saying hello.

1. I wonder why the boss was so irritable today.
be upset about something

2. I wonder why Pamela arrived late for work.
miss the bus

3. I wonder why Larry quit.
find a better job

4. I wonder why Donna went home early today.
be feeling "under the weather"

5. I wonder why Rover got sick last night.
eat something he shouldn't have

7. I wonder why Diane went to sleep so early.
have a hard day at the office

9. I wonder why my computer shut down.
run out of power

11. I wonder why Mom got stopped by a police officer.
be driving too fast

13. I wonder why the minister arrived late for the wedding.
get lost

6. I wonder why Jill prepared so much food.
expect a lot of people to come to her party

8. I wonder why my shirt shrank* so much.
be 100 percent cotton

10. I wonder why my cactus plant died.
have a rare disease

12. I wonder why Dad got searched by the security person.
set off the metal detector

14.

*shrink - shrank - shrunk

READING

UNEXPECTED GUESTS

Melba had a very difficult situation at her house a few days ago. Her relatives from Minneapolis arrived unexpectedly, without any advance notice whatsoever, and they stayed for the entire weekend.

Needless to say, Melba was very upset. If she had known that her relatives from Minneapolis were going to arrive and stay for the entire weekend, she would have been prepared for their visit. She would have bought a lot of food. She would have cleaned the house. And she certainly wouldn't have invited all her daughter's friends from nursery school to come over and play.

Poor Melba! She really wishes her relatives had called in advance to say they were coming.

✔ READING CHECK-UP

TRUE, FALSE, OR MAYBE?

Answer True, False, or Maybe (if the answer isn't in the story).

1. Melba lives in Minneapolis.
2. Her relatives didn't call to say they were coming.
3. If Melba's relatives hadn't arrived unexpectedly, she would have been prepared for their visit.
4. When her relatives arrived, Melba was upset, but she didn't say so.
5. If her house had been clean and she had had more food, Melba would have been more prepared for her relatives' unexpected visit.
6. Melba's relatives realized they should have called in advance to say they were coming.

WHAT'S THE WORD?

Complete these sentences using *would have* or *wouldn't have* and the correct form of the verb.

1. If the plane had arrived on time, I (*be*) _____ late for the meeting.
2. If the weather had been nice yesterday, we (*go*) _____ to the beach.
3. If I hadn't been out of town, I (*miss*) _____ my daughter's soccer game.
4. If I had seen that stop sign, Officer, I certainly (*drive*) _____ through it.
5. If the president hadn't been in a hurry, he (*give*) _____ a longer speech.
6. If I had known you were a vegetarian, I (*make*) _____ beef stew.

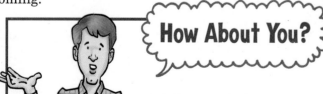 **How About You?** Have you ever had a difficult situation when something unexpected happened and you weren't prepared? Tell about it.

100

READING

WISHING IT HAD HAPPENED DIFFERENTLY

Andrew didn't save his work on his computer yesterday. He really wishes he had saved it. If he had saved it, he wouldn't have lost his history paper. And if he hadn't lost his history paper, he would have been able to hand it in on time today.

Marilyn's alarm clock didn't ring this morning. She really wishes it had rung. If it had rung, she wouldn't have been late for work this morning. And if she hadn't been late, her supervisor wouldn't have scolded her.

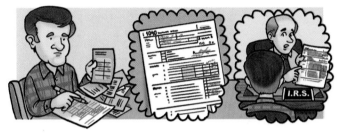

Stan filled out his income tax form very quickly this year. He really wishes he had filled it out more carefully. If he had filled it out more carefully, he wouldn't have made so many mistakes. And if he hadn't made so many mistakes, he wouldn't have gotten into trouble with the Internal Revenue Service.

Mr. and Mrs. Carson didn't follow the directions on the box when they baked cookies yesterday. They really wish they had. If they had followed the directions, they would have used the right ingredients. And if they had used the right ingredients, the cookies wouldn't have been as hard as rocks!

 READING *CHECK-UP*

TRUE, FALSE, OR MAYBE?

Answer True, False, or Maybe (if the answer isn't in the story).

1. Andrew handed in his history paper on time.
2. He wishes he had saved his work on his computer.
3. Marilyn's supervisor didn't scold her.
4. If Stan hadn't completed the form quickly, he wouldn't have made any mistakes.
5. Mr. and Mrs. Carson's cookies would have been softer if they hadn't used the wrong ingredients.

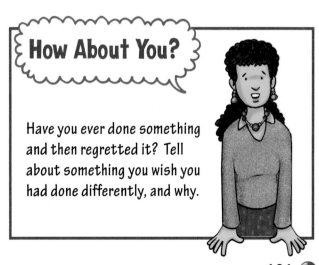

How About You?

Have you ever done something and then regretted it? Tell about something you wish you had done differently, and why.

101

I Wish

I **live** in Boston. I **wish** I **lived** in New York.	I **lived** in Boston. I **wish** I **had lived** in New York.

I don't know my neighbors. ☹️
I'm so lonely.

A. I wish I knew my neighbors.

B. Why do you say that?

A. If I knew my neighbors, I wouldn't be so lonely.

B. I know what you mean.

I didn't know how to get around town when I moved here. ☹️
I was so confused.

A. I wish I had known how to get around town when I moved here.

B. Why do you say that?

A. If I had known how to get around town when I moved here, I wouldn't have been so confused.

B. I know what you mean.

1. I don't drive to work. ☹️
I have to wait for the train every morning.

2. I didn't drive to work today. ☹️
I had to wait an hour for the bus.

3. I don't do daily exercises. ☹
I have to go on a diet.

4. I didn't do my homework last night. ☹
I had to do it early this morning.

5. I don't have a good job. ☹
I'm concerned about my future.

6. I didn't have a flu shot last fall. ☹
I was sick all winter.

7. I'm not an optimist. ☹
I get depressed so often.

8. I wasn't prepared for my math test. ☹
I got a low grade.

9. My husband and I don't take dance lessons. ☹
We feel "out of place" at parties.

10. I didn't take medicine when my tooth began to hurt. ☹
I felt miserable all day.

How to Say It!

Empathizing

> I know what you mean.

> I know *exactly* what you mean.

> I know what you're saying.

> I know *exactly* what you're saying.

> I understand what you're saying.

> I understand.

Here are some other expressions people use in different places:
I hear you. I hear what you're saying. I can relate (to that).

Practice the conversations in this lesson again. Use different expressions for empathizing.

103

RUMORS

All the people at the office are talking about Samantha these days. There's a rumor that Samantha is going to be transferred to the company's office in Paris, and everybody is convinced that the rumor is true. After all, if she weren't going to be transferred to the company's office in Paris, she wouldn't have put her condo up for sale. She wouldn't have started taking French lessons. And she DEFINITELY wouldn't have broken up with her boyfriend.

Of course, the people at the office don't know for sure whether Samantha is going to be transferred to the company's office in Paris. It's only a rumor. They'll just have to wait and see.

All the assembly-line workers at the National Motors automobile company are worrying about the future these days. There's a rumor that the factory is going to close down soon, and everybody is convinced that the rumor is true. After all, if the factory weren't going to close down soon, everybody on the night shift wouldn't have been laid off. The managers wouldn't all be reading the want ads and working on their resumes. And the boss DEFINITELY wouldn't have canceled the annual company picnic!

Of course, the assembly-line workers at National Motors don't know for sure whether the factory is going to close down soon. It's only a rumor. They'll just have to wait and see.

✔ READING *CHECK-UP*

TRUE, FALSE, OR MAYBE?

Answer True, False, or Maybe (if the answer isn't in the story).

1. Samantha is going to be transferred to the company's office in Paris.
2. Samantha hasn't put her condo up for sale.
3. The people at the office think Samantha wouldn't have broken up with her boyfriend if she weren't going to be transferred.
4. There's a rumor that workers on the night shift at the National Motors factory are going to lose their jobs.
5. There isn't going to be a company picnic this year.
6. The factory is going to close down soon.

1. The students in our class were upset when our teacher quit last week.
    a. We won't be upset if she doesn't quit.
    b. We wouldn't be upset if she didn't quit.
    c. We wouldn't have been upset if she hadn't quit.

2. I didn't come over to your table and have lunch with you because I didn't see you in the cafeteria.
    a. If I saw you, I would have come over and had lunch with you.
    b. If I had seen you, I would have come over and had lunch with you.
    c. If I had seen you, I would come over and have lunch with you.

3. I'm afraid I can't help you type those letters because I'm going to leave work early today.
    a. If I weren't going to leave work early, I'd help you type those letters.
    b. If I were going to leave work early, I'd help you type those letters.
    c. If I were going to leave work early, I wouldn't help you type those letters.

4. Betsy didn't take her umbrella to work today. She got wet on the way home.
    a. If she hadn't taken her umbrella to work, she wouldn't have gotten wet.
    b. If she had taken her umbrella to work, she wouldn't have gotten wet.
    c. If she hadn't taken her umbrella to work, she would have gotten wet.

LISTENING

Listen and choose the statement that is true based on what you hear.

1. a. She's rich.
   b. She isn't rich.

2. a. He remembered her e-mail address.
   b. He didn't remember her e-mail address.

3. a. They would have enjoyed the game more if they had had better seats.
   b. They wouldn't have enjoyed the game more if they had had better seats.

4. a. The boys in the hallway aren't the landlord's children.
   b. The boys in the hallway are the landlord's children.

5. a. He wasn't hired for the job.
   b. He was hired for the job.

6. a. Johnny's grandparents are at his party.
   b. Johnny's grandparents couldn't come to his party.

IN YOUR OWN WORDS

FOR WRITING AND DISCUSSION

Have you heard any rumors lately at school or at work? Tell a story about a rumor.

What's the rumor?
Do you think the rumor is true?
Why or why not?

I hope it's sunny tomorrow.   *(It might be sunny.)*

I wish it were sunny.   *(It isn't sunny.)*

I wish it had been sunny   *(It wasn't sunny.)*
    during our picnic.

Practice these conversations.

1.

2.

3.

What do **you** hope? What do **you** wish? Share your thoughts with other students.

PRONUNCIATION Reduced *have*

Listen. Then say it.

They would have enjoyed their vacation.

He wouldn't have arrived late.

She would have taken her umbrella.

I wouldn't have quit.

Say it. Then listen.

We would have used the right ingredients.

They wouldn't have invited so many people.

He would have been on time.

It wouldn't have shrunk.

Write in your journal about something in your life that you wish you had done, but didn't. What do you wish you had done? Why? What would have happened in your life if you had done that?

CHAPTER SUMMARY

GRAMMAR

PAST UNREAL CONDITIONAL (IF___WOULD HAVE)

If	I he she we you they	had known,	I he she we you they	**would have** told them.

If	I he she we you they	hadn't missed the bus,	I he she we you they	**wouldn't have** been late.

WISH-CLAUSES

I We You They	wish	I we you they	had gone there. hadn't gone there.
He She	wishes	he she	

I live in New York.
I wish I lived in California.

I don't know my neighbors.
I wish I knew my neighbors.

I lived in Boston.
I wish I had lived in Miami.

I didn't do that.
I wish I had done that.

KEY VOCABULARY

NOUNS

alarm clock
assembly line
audience
automobile factory
cactus plant
chemistry set
condo
cotton
disease
encore
flu shot
income tax form
metal detector

minister
mood
mortgage
nursery school
optimist
performance
postcard
printer
relatives
rumor
school play
snowman
traffic light
wedding dress

VERBS

close down
expect
get searched
get stopped
hand in
perform
run by
save
scold
set off
shrink
shut down
take lessons
trust

ADJECTIVES

confused
convinced
irritable
lonely
miserable
prepared
rare

EXPRESSIONS

have a hard day
out of place
put up for sale
run out of
set on fire
under the weather

Reported Speech
Sequence of Tenses

- Reporting What People Have Said
- Reporting Information
- Expressing Surprise
- Indicating Lack of Prior Knowledge
- Leaving, Taking, and Conveying Messages

- Job Interviews
- Asking for and Giving Reasons
- Discussing Feelings
- Advice

VOCABULARY PREVIEW

1. bride
2. groom
3. interviewer
4. movie star
5. school-bus driver

6. college entrance exam
7. dictionary
8. engine
9. lion
10. message

11. navy
12. pipe
13. puppy
14. radiator
15. robbery

What Did She Say?

"**I'm** busy."		**he was** busy.
"**I'm working** hard."		**he was working** hard.
"**I like** jazz."		**he liked** jazz.
"**I'm going to** buy a new car."		**he was going to** buy a new car.
"**I went** to Paris last year."	He said (that)*	**he had gone** to Paris last year.
"**I was** in London last week."		**he had been** in London last week.
"**I've seen** the movie."		**he had seen** the movie.
"**I'll call** the doctor."		**he would call** the doctor.
"**I can** help you."		**he could** help me.

I'm sick.

A. I forgot to tell you. Grandma called yesterday.

B. Really? What did she say?

A. She said (that)* **she was sick**.

A. I forgot to tell you. _____ called yesterday.

B. Really? What did _____ say?

A. _____ said (that)*_____.

We're engaged.

1. *Miguel and Maria*

I'm doing very well in college this semester.

2. *Robert*

* Or: "He / She / They told me (that)"

3. *Aunt Margaret*

4. *our upstairs neighbors*

5. *our niece Terry*

6. *Uncle Ted*

7. *your brother in Detroit*

8. *your sister in Seattle*

9. *the woman from the furniture store*

10. *the TV repairman*

11. *my boss*

12. *our nephew Paul*

13. *the little girl down the street*

14. *the auto mechanic*

15. *my boyfriend*

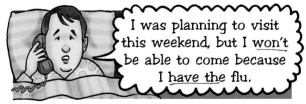

16. *Uncle Frank*

He had been planning to

He wouldn't

He had the flu

111

Haven't You Heard?

| John **is** sick. | I knew
I didn't know | (that) John **was** sick. |

A. What's everybody talking about?

B. Haven't you heard? Our English teacher is in the hospital!

A. You're kidding! I didn't know (that) our English teacher was in the hospital.

B. You didn't?! I thought EVERYBODY knew (that) our English teacher was in the hospital!

A. What's everybody _____ about?

B. Haven't you heard? _____!

A. You're kidding! I didn't know (that) _____.

B. You didn't?! I thought EVERYBODY knew (that) _____!

1. What's everybody talking about?

2. What's everybody so upset about?

3. What's everybody so happy about?

4. What's everybody so nervous about?

5. What's everybody so angry about?

6. What's everybody so happy about?

7. What's everybody so anxious about?

8. What's everybody so excited about?

9. What's everybody talking about?

10.

READING

A LOT OF MESSAGES

Sally was home alone this afternoon while her parents were at work. There were a lot of phone calls, and Sally wrote down a lot of messages.

Grandpa is feeling much better today.

Grandma

I haven't received this month's rent yet.

the landlord

I'll call back later.

Uncle Harry

We were robbed last night.

the neighbors across the street

I won't be able to fix the bathtub today because I'm sick.

the plumber

We fixed the radiator, but we've found something wrong with the engine.

Joe's Auto Repair Shop

Grandma called. She said Grandpa was feeling much better today.

The landlord called. He said he hadn't received this month's rent yet.

Uncle Harry called. He said he would call back later.

The neighbors across the street called. They said they had been robbed last night.

The plumber called. He said he wouldn't be able to fix the bathtub today because he was sick.

Joe's Auto Repair Shop called. They said they had fixed the radiator, but they had found something wrong with the engine.

✔ READING CHECK-UP

Q & A

The next day, Sally was home alone again. Her mother called from the office. Create dialogs based on the following model and information.

> A. Tell me, have there been any calls?
> B. Yes. _____ called.
> A. Oh? What did ___ say?
> B. ___ said _____.

1. Grandma • "Grandpa isn't feeling very well and wants me to call the doctor."
2. The landlord • "I received your check this morning."
3. Uncle Harry • "I'm getting married next month, and I want all of you to come to my wedding."
4. The neighbors across the street • "The police caught the man who robbed our house."
5. The plumber • "I'm still sick, and I can't get there today."
6. Joe's Auto Repair Shop • "We've finished working on the engine, and the car is ready to be picked up."

COMPLETE THE STORY

Well, . . .

Your brother got engaged.

Your sister and brother-in-law are going to have a baby.

Your father is planning to retire next month.

There was a big fire at the high school.

The dog had six puppies.

And your high school sweetheart married a movie star and moved to Hollywood.

Aside from that, not much else happened.

Hi, Mom! What's new?

HOME FROM THE NAVY

Bill serves as a lieutenant in the navy. He returned home last weekend after being at sea for several months. Since he hadn't been in touch with his family for a long time, he was very surprised at all the things that had happened while he was away.

He didn't know his brother <u>had gotten</u> 1 engaged. He also didn't know his sister and brother-in-law _____ 2 have a baby. And he was unaware that his father _____ 3 retire next month.

In addition, he didn't know there _____ 4 a big fire at the high school. He hadn't heard that the dog _____ 5 six puppies. And he had no idea that his high school sweetheart _____ 6 a movie star and _____ 7 to Hollywood.

A lot of things certainly had changed while Bill was away.

TRUE, FALSE, OR MAYBE?

Answer True, False, or Maybe (if the answer isn't in the story).

1. Bill has been on a ship for the past several months.
2. His sister had a baby while he was away.
3. His father has retired.
4. Bill's high school was very large.
5. Bill's former girlfriend lives in Hollywood now.

LISTENING

Listen and choose the statement that is true based on what you hear.

1. a. It snowed.
    b. It's still snowing.

2. a. He didn't know that his supervisor had been in the hospital.
    b. He didn't know that his supervisor was in the hospital.

3. a. She wasn't aware that jackets were on sale.
    b. She wasn't aware that jackets had been on sale.

4. a. He didn't know she had to work on Saturday.
    b. He didn't know she had worked on Saturday.

5. a. She was aware that Sherman had been thinking of leaving.
    b. She was unaware that Sherman had been thinking of leaving.

6. a. Her friends hadn't told her they were going to move.
    b. Her friends had told her they were going to move.

What Did They Ask?

"Where is the bank?"		where the bank was.
"When are you going to visit me?"		when I was going to visit him.
"Do you speak English?"	He asked me	{ if / whether } I spoke English.
"Have you seen Mary?"		{ if / whether } I had seen Mary.

A. You won't believe what a three-year-old boy asked me today!

B. What did he ask you?

A. He asked me why there was a Santa Claus in every department store in town.

B. I can't believe he asked you that!

A. I can't either.

A. You won't believe what my boss asked me today!

B. What did she ask you?

A. She asked me { if / whether } I wanted to receive a raise this year.

B. I can't believe she asked you that!

A. I can't either.

1. *my history teacher*

2. *my boyfriend*

3. *my nine-year-old nephew*

4. *the woman at my job interview*

5. *my students*

6. *my parents*

(continued)

7. *my philosophy professor*

8. *my daughter*

9. *my basketball coach*

10. *my son*

11. *a taxi driver*

12. *the patient in Room 12*

13. *Grandma*

14.

THE JOB INTERVIEW

Charles had a job interview a few days ago at the United Insurance Company. The interview lasted almost an hour, and Charles had to answer a lot of questions.

First, the interviewer asked Charles where he had gone to school. Then she asked if he had had any special training. She asked where he had worked. She also asked whether he was willing to move to another city. She wanted to know if he could work overtime and weekends. She asked him how his health was. She asked him whether he had ever been fired. She wanted to know why he had had four different jobs last year.

And finally, the interviewer asked the most difficult question. She wanted to know why Charles thought he was more qualified for the position than the other sixty-two people who had applied.

Charles had never been asked so many questions at a job interview before. He doesn't know how well he did, but he tried his best.

The questions in the illustration:

Where did you go to school?

Have you had any special training?

Where have you worked?

Are you willing to move to another city?

Can you work overtime and weekends?

How is your health?

Have you ever been fired?

Why did you have four different jobs last year?

Why do you think you're more qualified for the position than the other sixty-two people who have applied?

✓ READING *CHECK-UP*

ROLE PLAY

You're applying for a job at the United Insurance Company. Role-play a job interview with another student, using the questions in the illustration as a guide.

How About You?

Tell about a job interview you had.
  Where was the interview?
  How long did it last?
  What questions did the interviewer ask?
  What were your answers?
  What was the most difficult question, and how did you answer it?
  Did you get the job?

Job interviewers sometimes like to ask difficult questions. Why do you think they do this? What are some difficult questions interviewers might ask? Make a list, and think of answers to those questions.

What Did They Tell You?

"Call me after five o'clock." "Stop complaining!" "Don't worry!" "Don't call me before nine o'clock."	to call him after five o'clock. to stop complaining. not to worry. not to call him before nine o'clock.

He told me {

Keep your dog in the house!
I'm afraid to deliver your mail!

A. I'm a little annoyed at the mailman.

B. How come?

A. He told me to keep my dog in the house.

B. Why did he tell you that?

A. He said (that) he was afraid to deliver my mail.

Don't play your music so loud!
You're bothering us!

A. I'm a little annoyed at my neighbors.

B. How come?

A. They told me not to play my music so loud.

B. Why did they tell you that?

A. They said (that) I was bothering them.

A. I'm a little annoyed at _____.
B. How come?
A. ____ told me _____.
B. Why did ____ tell you that?
A. ____ said (that) _____.

1. *my doctor*

2. *my dentist*

3. *my math teacher*

4. *the school-bus driver*

5. *my girlfriend*

6. *my parents*

7. *my boss*

8. *my landlord*

9. *my seven-year-old son*

How About You?

Do you remember the last time someone said something that really annoyed you?

What did the person say? (He/She told me . . .)
Why do you think he/she said that?
Did you say anything back?

121

GOOD ADVICE

Margaret had a bad stomachache yesterday afternoon. She called her doctor and asked him what she should do. Her doctor told her to rest in bed. He also told her not to eat too much for dinner. And he told her to call him in the morning if she was still sick. Margaret felt better after speaking with her doctor. She's glad she can always depend on him for good advice.

Eric went out on his first date yesterday evening. Before he left the house, he asked his parents if they had any advice. They told him to be polite when he met the girl's mother and father. They also told him not to drive too fast. And they told him not to bring his date home later than ten o'clock. Eric felt more prepared for his date after speaking to his parents. He's glad he can always depend on them for good advice.

Mrs. Tanaka's students are going to take the college entrance examination this Saturday, and they're very nervous. They asked Mrs. Tanaka if she had any helpful advice. She told them to answer the questions carefully. She also told them not to spend too much time on a question that was too difficult. And she told them to get a good night's sleep the night before the examination. Mrs. Tanaka's students felt more confident after speaking with her. They're glad they can always depend on her for good advice.

Mr. and Mrs. Pratt are going away on vacation soon, and they're concerned because there have been several robberies in their neighborhood recently. They called the police and asked them what they could do to prevent their house from being broken into while they were away. The police told them to lock all the windows and leave on a few lights. They also advised them to ask the neighbors to pick up the mail. And they warned them not to tell too many people that they would be away. Mr. and Mrs. Pratt felt reassured after speaking with the police. They're glad they can always depend on them for good advice.

✔ READING CHECK-UP

TRUE, FALSE, OR MAYBE?

Answer True, False, or Maybe (if the answer isn't in the story).

1. Margaret told her doctor to rest in bed.
2. Margaret didn't eat very much for dinner yesterday.
3. Eric hadn't gone out on a date before yesterday.
4. Eric brought his date home by ten o'clock.
5. Mrs. Tanaka teaches at a college.
6. Mrs. Tanaka got a good night's sleep the night before the examination.
7. Locking windows and leaving on lights are two ways to prevent robberies.
8. The Pratts' house was broken into while they were away.

CHOOSE

1. Eric's parents told him _____.
   a. not to drive too fast
   b. don't drive too fast

2. Mrs. Tanaka told her students _____.
   a. answer the questions carefully
   b. to answer the questions carefully

3. She told him _____.
   a. don't worry
   b. not to worry

4. She asked _____ a vegetarian.
   a. if I was
   b. whether are you

5. My friends said that _____.
   a. they will be here
   b. they would be here

6. We _____ them to call us.
   a. said
   b. told

PRONUNCIATION Reduced *to*

Listen. Then say it.

He told me to sit down.

She told me not to call her.

She asked me where I went to school.

They said they wouldn't be able to come to the party.

Say it. Then listen.

She told me to lose some weight.

He told me not to eat candy.

He asked me if I wanted to get married.

She said I didn't have to work overtime.

Write in your journal about a time when you needed advice. Why did you need advice? (What was the situation?) Who did you ask for advice? What did you ask? What did the person tell you? Did you follow the person's advice? Was it good advice or bad advice? Why?

GRAMMAR

REPORTED SPEECH
SEQUENCE OF TENSES

"I'm busy."		**he was** busy.
"I **like** jazz."		**he liked** jazz.
"I'm **going to** buy a new car."		**he was going to** buy a new car.
"I **went** to Paris last year."	He said (that)	**he had gone** to Paris last year.
"I **was** in London last week."		**he had been** in London last week.
"I've **seen** the movie."		**he had seen** the movie.
"I'll **call** the doctor."		**he would call** the doctor.
"I **can** help you."		**he could** help me.

John **is** sick.		John **was** sick.
Jack **is** going to be a father.	I knew (that)	Jack **was** going to be a father.
Our landlord **wants** to sell the building.	I didn't know (that)	our landlord **wanted** to sell the building.
We **can't** use our dictionaries.		we **couldn't** use our dictionaries.

"Where is the bank?"		where the bank was.
"When are you going to visit me?"		when I was going to visit him.
"Do you speak English?"	He asked me	{ if / whether } I spoke English.
"Have you seen Mary?"		{ if / whether } I had seen Mary.

"Call me after five o'clock."		to call him after five o'clock.
"Stop complaining!"		to stop complaining.
"Don't worry!"	He told me	not to worry.
"Don't call me before nine o'clock."		not to call him before nine o'clock.

KEY VOCABULARY

NOUNS		VERBS		ADJECTIVES
advice	movie star	advise	dye	annoyed
bride	navy	apply	escape	confident
college entrance exam	pipe	bother	kiss	engaged
dictionary	position	cancel	leave on	prepared
engine	puppy	clog	lock	professional
grease	radiator	deliver	pour	qualified
groom	robber	depend	prevent	reassured
interviewer	school-bus driver	disturb		unaware
lion	training			willing
message				

Feature Article
Fact File
Around the World
Interview
We've Got Mail!

SIDE by SIDE Gazette

Global Exchange
Listening
Fun with Idioms
What Are They
Saying?

Volume 4   Number 3

Polish Up Your Interview Skills!

Tips from the experts

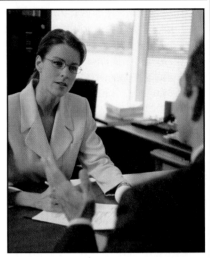

Going to a job interview can be a very challenging experience. A lot of people are probably applying for the same job. What can you do to make a good impression and stand out from the crowd?

The experts say, "Be prepared!" Learn about the company before your interview. Find out about the company's products or services. Read about the company in the newspaper, or try to find information on the Internet. (Many companies have their own websites with lots of information.) Also, dress appropriately for the interview. Don't wear casual clothes. Dress neatly and conservatively.

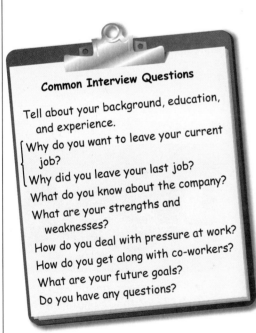

Common Interview Questions

Tell about your background, education, and experience.
Why do you want to leave your current job?
Why did you leave your last job?
What do you know about the company?
What are your strengths and weaknesses?
How do you deal with pressure at work?
How do you get along with co-workers?
What are your future goals?
Do you have any questions?

Prepare in advance for the types of questions you will probably be asked. The interviewer will most likely ask you to tell about your background, education, and experience. If you are employed, the interviewer may ask you why you want to leave your current job. Or, if you aren't employed at the time of the interview, the interviewer might ask why you left your last job. You should be prepared to talk about what you know about the company. Don't be surprised if you are asked what your strengths and weaknesses are. Be ready to answer questions about how you deal with pressure at work. An interviewer will most likely ask you how you get along with co-workers. You may also be asked what your future goals are. And don't forget that the interviewer will probably ask if you have any questions.

Be sure to answer the interviewer's questions honestly. Try to show that you are motivated, responsible, and very interested in the job. Be confident, but don't brag about yourself. (Don't say how great you are. Instead, give examples of things you've done that show your strengths.)

Be prepared for when the interviewer asks if you have any questions. You can ask about the job responsibilities, the company in general, when the position will be filled, and other things. Some experts say that it isn't a good idea to ask too many questions about salary, vacations, or benefits during the first interview. If the company has follow-up interviews for the position, that might be a better time for such questions. Before you leave the interview, make sure you know the names and titles of all the people you met. Write a thank-you letter to the interviewer as soon as possible. Say thank you for the interviewer's time, describe why you think you're the right person for the job, and offer to go back for another interview if they want you to.

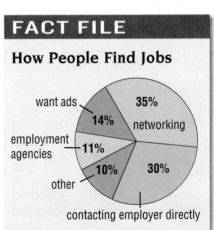

FACT FILE

How People Find Jobs

want ads
14%
employment agencies
11%
other
10%
35% networking
30%
contacting employer directly

Who Got the Job?

Sarah Jones went to a job interview yesterday at a computer software company. First, the interviewer asked her about her background and experience. She told about where she had gone to school, what she had studied, and what kinds of jobs she had had. When the interviewer asked her why she wanted to leave her current job, she said that she was looking for a more challenging position. Then the interviewer asked Sarah what she knew about the company. She answered that she used some of the company's software and she had read articles about the company in the newspaper. Then the interviewer asked what her strengths and weaknesses were. She replied that she worked very hard and got along well with people, but she had some problems writing business letters. She explained that she was now taking a business writing class at a local college. Finally, the interviewer asked Sarah if she had any questions. Sarah asked if the job required a lot of travel, and she asked what the company's plans for the future were. As soon as she got home, Sarah wrote a thank-you note to the interviewer.

Bob Mills went to a job interview yesterday at the same company. First, the interviewer asked him about his background and experience. Bob said he had listed all that information on his resume and the interviewer could find it there. When the interviewer asked him why he wanted to change employers, Bob replied that he was looking for a job with shorter hours and fewer responsibilities. Then the interviewer asked what he knew about the company. Bob said he wasn't really familiar with the company's products, and he asked what they were. When the interviewer asked what his strengths and weaknesses were, Bob said he hadn't really thought about that before, but it was a good question. Finally, the interviewer asked Bob if he had any questions. Bob asked if he could have 25 vacation days during his first year, and he wanted to know whether he would be able to bring his dog to the office every day. Bob went home feeling good about the interview. He thought it had gone well, and he waited for the company to call.

Who do you think got the job? For fun, act out the two interviews!

AROUND THE WORLD

Job Interviews

Job interviews can be very different around the world. An interviewer's questions, the "body language" that should be used, and the formality of an interview vary from country to country.

If you're at a job interview in Japan, don't look directly into the eyes of the interviewer. It is considered rude. But if you're at an interview in the United States, you should definitely make eye contact with the interviewer. If you don't, the interviewer may think you aren't trustworthy or confident.

In the United States and some other countries, interviewers aren't supposed to ask questions about family, marital status, and other personal information. In most countries, however, personal questions are very common during job interviews.

In France, shake hands with the interviewer lightly, not firmly. In many other countries, you should shake hands firmly, because a firm handshake is a sign of confidence. In Germany, your interview might begin with a very short informal conversation followed by a formal interview. In Mexico and many other countries, the informal small talk might take longer, and in some cases the entire interview might be informal.

What are job interviews like in countries you know?

Interview

A **Side by Side Gazette** *reporter recently interviewed Monica Salinas, a Human Resources manager for a large insurance company. As a job interviewer, Ms. Salinas reads thousands of resumes and interviews hundreds of people each year.*

Q. Tell us about your job.

A. I'm responsible for interviewing applicants for all the available positions in our company. Our firm is very large, so we receive more than 50 resumes and interview up to ten people each day. It's a lot of work!

Q. What are your favorite interview questions?

A. I like to ask applicants how they think other people would describe them. I also like to ask about weekend activities, hobbies, and other things that help me get to know the applicant as a person.

Q. What was your most memorable interview?

A. It was with a young woman from Brazil. She had only been in this country for four years. When she arrived, she didn't speak a word of English. But at her interview, her English was excellent! She said she had taken English courses and then studied business at a community college. She said she was the first person from her family to go to college. She impressed me so much. I asked her how she could contribute to our company. She said she would be the hardest worker here. Well, she is! I hired her, and last month she was chosen "Employee of the Year" and received a big bonus check. I asked her what she was going to do with the extra money. She said that she had already sent it to her family in Brazil so they could start building a new home.

Q. Have you had any unusual interviews?

A. One applicant said he was hungry. He opened a paper bag, took out a sandwich, and ate during the entire interview! Another time, an applicant was so nervous that she fainted. I got her some water, and I offered to reschedule the interview. She was lying on the floor, but she said that she was okay and wanted to continue. So I sat with her on the floor, and we had a very nice conversation.

Q. What is your best piece of advice for someone going to a job interview?

A. Be yourself! Smile, relax, and be honest. Let the interviewer see who you really are.

FUN with IDIOMS

Do You Know These Expressions?

____ 1. Don't put your foot in your mouth!

____ 2. Don't talk the interviewer's head off!

____ 3. Don't inflate your resume!

____ 4. Don't beat around the bush!

a. Answer questions briefly!

b. Answer questions directly!

c. Don't say the wrong thing!

d. Don't exaggerate your skills or experience!

We've Got Mail!

Dear Side by Side,

I have a question about tenses and reported speech. I understand that this is the correct way to say each of these sentences:

He said (that) he **was** hungry.

She told me (that) she **was** sick.

They said (that) they **were** engaged.

However, I often hear English speakers say:

He said (that) he **is** hungry.

She told me (that) she **is** sick.

They said (that) they **are** engaged.

Are both ways correct? I'm very confused.

Sincerely,

"Tense About Reported Speech"

Dear "Tense About Reported Speech,"

The first way to say these sentences is grammatically correct. However, in informal speech, the second way is also correct, especially when the person is reporting about something that someone has just said. We also "break the rule" when we talk about facts that are always true. For example:

We knew (that) Paris **is** the capital of France.

The teacher said (that) the Amazon **is** the longest river.

We hope this answers your question. Thanks for writing.

Sincerely,

Side by Side

Global Exchange

BillG: You won't believe what my neighbor in the apartment across the hall told me today! She said I was the noisiest person in our building! She told me that I played the drums too loud at night. She said that I had too many parties on weekends. And she asked me if I knew that dogs weren't allowed in the building. I told her that she had made a mistake, and that she had mixed me up with our neighbor down the hall. After all, I don't play the drums, I never have parties, and I don't have a dog! She apologized, and we had a nice conversation after that. I told her that if she wanted, I would go with her to talk to our noisy neighbor. That should be an interesting conversation!

Send a message to a keypal. Tell about an interesting conversation you have had.

What Are They Saying?

LISTENING

You have six messages!

You Have Six Messages!

① **a.** Jim Gavin wanted to know why money had been taken out of his paycheck.
  b. Jim Gavin wanted to know why money hadn't been taken out of his paycheck.

② **a.** Denise said she hadn't been able to go to the meeting.
  b. Denise said she wouldn't be able to go to the meeting.

③ **a.** Patty told Joe that she had ordered more pens.
  b. Patty told Joe that she had canceled the order for pens.

④ **a.** Jane Adams called to say that the painters hadn't arrived yet.
  b. Jane Adams called to tell Joe when the painters would arrive.

⑤ **a.** George asked Joe if he could go to a doctor's appointment tomorrow morning.
  b. George told Joe that he would be at a doctor's appointment tomorrow morning.

⑥ **a.** Michelle told Joe she had taken a job with another company.
  b. Michelle told Joe that another company had offered her a job.

Tag Questions
Emphatic Sentences

- Verifying
- Expressing Surprise
- Reporting Information
- Congratulating
- Initiating Topics

- Expressing Opinions
- Expressing Agreement
- Writing a Personal Letter
- Writing a Business Memo
- Performance on the Job

VOCABULARY PREVIEW

1. couple
2. dolphin
3. kite
4. memo

5. moon
6. spare tire
7. toaster
8. wagon

9. engaged
10. overcooked
11. punctual
12. scary

This Is the Bus to the Zoo, Isn't It?

Ken **is** here, **isn't** he?
You **were** sick, **weren't** you?
Maria **will** be here soon, **won't** she?
Timmy **has** gone to bed, **hasn't** he?

I **am** on time, **aren't** I?

You like ice cream, **don't** you?
Ed worked yesterday, **didn't** he?

A. This is the bus to the zoo, isn't it?

B. Yes, it is.

A. That's what I thought.

1. Neil Armstrong was the first person on the moon, *wasn't he*?

2. I can skateboard here, ____? *couldn't I / cann't I*

3. Ms. Lee will be on vacation next week, ____? *won't she?*

4. It's going to rain today, ____? *isn't it*

5. We've already seen this movie, ____? *haven't we*

6. I'm on time for my interview, ____? *Aren't*

7. You work in the Shipping Department, ____? *don't you*

8. You locked the front door, ____? *didn't you*

9. You're a famous movie star, ____? *aren't you*

130

This TV Isn't On Sale This Week, Is It?

Bill **isn't** here, **is** he?
You **weren't** angry, **were** you?
Nina **won't** be upset, **will** she?
You **haven't** eaten, **have** you?
I**'m not** late, **am** I?

Mark **doesn't** ski, **does** he?
They **didn't** leave, **did** they?

A. This TV isn't on sale this week, is it?

B. No, it isn't.

A. That's what I thought.

---

1. There weren't any computers when you were young, _____? *were there*

2. I can't fish here, _____? *Can I*

3. Mr. Martinez won't be in the office tomorrow, _____? *will he*

4. You aren't really going to go swimming, _____? *are you*

5. The mail hasn't come yet, _____? *has it*

6. I'm not allowed to park here, _____? *am I*

7. The children don't use this old wagon anymore, _____? *do they*

8. We didn't have a homework assignment yesterday, _____? *did we*

9. I haven't taught "tag questions" before, _____? *have I*

I'm Really Surprised!

A. You like spaghetti, don't you?

B. Actually, I don't.

A. You DON'T?! I'm really surprised!
I was SURE you liked spaghetti!

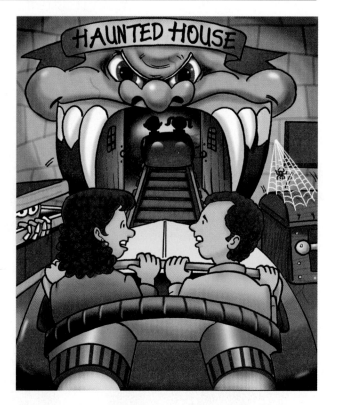

A. This ride isn't scary, is it?

B. Actually, it is.

A. It IS?! I'm really surprised!
I was SURE this ride wasn't scary!

1. It's going to be a nice day tomorrow,
_____?

3. This building has an elevator, _____?
doesn't it?

2. I don't have to wear a jacket and tie
here, _____? do I

4. You can swim, _____? Can't you.

If doesn't
it.

you could swim

5. The bank hasn't closed yet, _____ has it_____?

6. I did well on the exam, _____? didn't I

7. I'm going to play today, _____? aren't you.

8. Dolphins can't talk, _____?

9. I wasn't going over fifty-five miles per hour, _____? Was I I had been going over

10. We have a spare tire, _____?

11. You aren't allergic to fish, _____ Are? you. You were not allergic

12. I'm not a suspect, _____?

How to Say It!

Expressing Surprise

I'm really surprised!

I'm very surprised!

That's very surprising!

I can't believe it!

I don't believe it!

Practice the conversations in this lesson again. Express surprise in different ways.

Congratulations!

A. I have some good news.

B. What is it?

A. My wife and I are celebrating our fiftieth wedding anniversary tomorrow!

B. You ARE?!

A. Yes, we are.

B. I don't believe it! You aren't REALLY celebrating your fiftieth wedding anniversary tomorrow, are you?

A. Yes, it's true. We ARE.

B. Well, congratulations! I'm very glad to hear that.

A. I have some good news.

B. What is it?

A. I just got a big raise!

B. You DID?!

A. Yes, I did.

B. I don't believe it! You didn't REALLY get a big raise, did you?

A. Yes, it's true. I DID.

B. Well, congratulations! I'm very glad to hear that!

1. I'm going to have a baby!

2. We won the basketball championship!

3. I've been promoted!

4. I can tie my shoes by myself!

5. My son is going to be in the Olympics!

6. I got a perfect score on the SAT test! *you did*

7. Steven Steelberg wants me to star in his new movie! *he does*

8. I've been invited to perform at the White House! *you have?*

9. I was interviewed by *Time* Magazine yesterday! *You were.*

10. My daughter has been accepted at Harvard University! *she has?*

11. I've discovered a cure for the common cold! *you have?*

12.

135

You're Right!

George was angry.	George WAS angry, wasn't he!
I'm late.	I AM late, aren't I!
They aren't very friendly.	They AREN'T very friendly, are they!
I don't know the answer.	I DON'T know the answer, do I!
They work hard.	They DO work hard, don't they!
John looks tired.	John DOES look tired, doesn't he!
Janet came late to class.	Janet DID come late to class, didn't she!

A. You know . . . the color blue looks very good on you.

B. You're right! The color blue DOES look very good on me, doesn't it!

A. You know . . . it isn't a very good day to fly a kite.

B. You're right!   It ISN'T a very good day to fly a kite, is it!

1. . . . you work too hard.

2. . . . Charlie is a very talented dog.

3. . . . Aunt Betty hasn't called in a long time.

4. ... you're playing this song too slowly.

5. ... this milk tastes sour.

6. ... these hamburgers are overcooked.

7. ... you have quite a few gray hairs.

8. ... you've been online for a long time.

9. ... we really shouldn't be playing frisbee here.

10. ... Peter looks just like his father.

11. ... children these days don't dress very neatly.

12. ... you missed a few spots.

13. ... Ms. Taylor gave us a lot of homework yesterday.

14. ... I won't be able to play in the game tomorrow.

15. ... your brother and my sister would make a nice couple.

16. ... this new toaster doesn't work very well.

17. ... Howard was a very generous person.

18.

READING

A BROKEN ENGAGEMENT

Dear John,

It's been a long time since I've written to you, hasn't it! I'm sorry it has taken me such a long time to write, but I really don't know where to begin this letter. You see, John, things have been very difficult since you took that job overseas several months ago. It has been very difficult for me to be engaged to somebody who is four thousand miles away, so I've decided that things have got to change.

I've decided to move out of my parents' house.

I'm going to get my own apartment.

I've started dating other guys.

I want to break our engagement.

And I gave your mother back the ring you had given me.

I'm sorry things have to end this way. You DO understand why I must do this, don't you?

Sincerely,
Jane

Dear Jane,

I received your letter today, and when I opened it I was shocked. I couldn't believe what you had written.

You haven't really decided to move out of your parents' house, have you?

You aren't really going to get your own apartment, are you?

You haven't really started dating other guys, have you?

You don't really want to break our engagement, do you?

And you didn't really give my mother back the ring I had given you, did you?

Please answer me as soon as possible!

Love,
John

P.S. You DO still love me, don't you?

Dear John,

    I HAVE decided to move out of my parents' house.

    I AM going to get my own apartment.

    I HAVE started dating other guys.

    I DO want to break our engagement.

    And I DID give your mother back the ring you had given me.

    I know this must hurt, but I DO have to be honest with you, don't I! I hope that someday you will understand.

                Good-bye,
                Jane

 READING *CHECK-UP*

WHAT'S THE ANSWER?

1. Why did Jane decide to break her engagement to John?
2. Where has Jane been living?
3. What did Jane do with the ring that John had given her?
4. How did John feel when he received Jane's first letter?
5. Did Jane realize how John would feel when he received her second letter?

CHOOSE

1. John wanted to know if Jane _____ to break their engagement.
   a. had really decided
   b. has really decided

2. John asked Jane whether she _____ her own apartment.
   a. had really gotten
   b. was really going to get

3. In her first letter, Jane said she _____ break their engagement.
   a. wants to
   b. wanted to

4. John was hoping she _____ him.
   a. still loved
   b. had still loved

5. In Jane's second letter, she told John she really _____ to move out of her parents' house.
   a. has decided
   b. had decided

6. She told him she hoped that someday he _____.
   a. would have understood
   b. would understand

IN YOUR OWN WORDS

FOR WRITING AND DISCUSSION

John is willing to do anything he can to save his relationship with Jane. He has some ideas about how to do this, and he's going to write to her one more time. Write John's letter to Jane.

UNFAIR ACCUSATIONS

```
To:  Michael Parker
From:  Ms. Lewis
Re:  Your performance at work

I'm concerned about your performance at work.

    You have been working too slowly.
    You often get to work late.
    You took too many vacation days last month.
    You aren't very polite to the customers.
    And you don't get along well with the other employees.

I'd like to meet with you as soon as possible to discuss this.
```

Michael's boss, Ms. Lewis, sent him a memo recently about his performance at work. In the memo, she said he had been working too slowly. She also said that he often got to work late. In addition, she observed that he had taken too many vacation days last month. She also mentioned that he wasn't very polite to the customers. And finally, she complained that he didn't get along well with the other employees.

When Michael got the memo, he was very upset. He feels that his boss is making unfair accusations. Michael feels that he HASN'T been working too slowly. He also feels that he DOESN'T often get to work late. In Michael's opinion, he DIDN'T take too many vacation days last month. He thinks he IS very polite to the customers. And he maintains that he DOES get along well with the other employees.

Michael realizes that he and his boss see things VERY differently, and he plans to speak to her about this as soon as possible.

✓ READING *CHECK-UP*

MATCH

Match the descriptions of job performance on the left with their meanings.

___ 1. punctual
___ 2. honest
___ 3. efficient
___ 4. industrious
___ 5. cooperative
___ 6. friendly
___ 7. considerate
___ 8. dedicated

a. pleasant and outgoing
b. easy to work with
c. works quickly and accurately
d. thoughtful of others
e. tells the truth
f. gets to work on time
g. cares about the work
h. works hard

LISTENING

Listen and decide who is speaking.

1. a. student – student
   b. student – teacher

2. a. tenant – tenant
   b. tenant – mail carrier

3. a. employee – employee
   b. student – student

4. a. salesperson – customer
   b. wife – husband

5. a. passenger – driver
   b. police officer – driver

6. a. doctor – nurse
   b. doctor – patient

IN YOUR OWN WORDS

FOR WRITING AND DISCUSSION

MEMO

To:
From:
Re:

Mr. Hopper is very pleased with Helen Baxter's performance at work. Using the story below as a guide, write a memo from Mr. Hopper to Helen Baxter.

POSITIVE FEEDBACK

Helen Baxter's boss, Mr. Hopper, sent her a memo recently about her job performance. He said that he was very pleased with her performance at work. He mentioned that she was very efficient and industrious. He observed that she got along well with her co-workers and customers. And he also said that she was very cooperative and considerate. Mr. Hopper wrote that the company had been so pleased with her work that they were going to give her a big raise.

INTERACTIONS

| He's She's It's | late, isn't | he! she! it! | We're You're They're | late, aren't | we! you! they! | I'm late, aren't I! |

A. You're tired, aren't you!

B. Tired? What makes you think I'm tired?

A. Well, you're falling asleep at the wheel.

B. Now that you mention it, I AM falling asleep at the wheel, aren't I!

A. You're nervous, aren't you!

B. Nervous? What makes you think I'm nervous?

A. Well, you haven't stopped pacing back and forth since early this morning.

B. Come to think of it, I HAVEN'T stopped pacing back and forth, have I!

A. You're in a bad mood, aren't you!

B. In a bad mood? What makes you think I'm in a bad mood?

A. Well, you shouted at me for no reason.

B. I guess I DID shout at you for no reason, didn't I!

142

A. You're _____, aren't you!

B. _____? What makes you think I'm _____?

A. Well, _____.

B. Now that you mention it,
Come to think of it, } _____, ____ ____!
I guess

Practice conversations with other students.

nervous

angry

tired

frightened

unhappy

bored

embarrassed

upset

jealous

How About You?

What do you do when you're nervous? angry? tired? frightened? unhappy? bored? embarrassed? upset? jealous?

143

Listen. Then say it.

Ken is here, isn't he?

You weren't angry, were you?

They DO work hard, don't they!

They AREN'T friendly, are they!

Say it. Then listen.

Timmy has gone to bed, hasn't he?

They didn't leave, did they?

He DOESN'T know the answer, does he!

That WAS an awful movie, wasn't it!

Have you ever received "positive feedback" about your performance at school, at work, in sports, or in other activities? What did people say? How did you feel after you received the positive feedback?

CHAPTER SUMMARY

GRAMMAR

TAG QUESTIONS

Ken **is** here, **isn't** he?
You **were** sick, **weren't** you?
Maria **will** be here soon, **won't** she?
Timmy **has** gone to bed, **hasn't** he?

I **am** on time, **aren't** I?

You like ice cream, **don't** you?
Ed worked yesterday, **didn't** he?

Bill **isn't** here, **is** he?
You **weren't** sick, **were** you?
Maria **won't** be here soon, **will** she?
Timmy **hasn't** gone to bed, **has** he?

I'**m not** late, **am** I?

You **don't** like ice cream, **do** you?
Ed **didn't** work yesterday, **did** he?

I'm We're You're They're	late,	aren't	I! we! you! they!
He's She's It's		isn't	he! she! it!

EMPHATIC SENTENCES

George was angry.
I'm late.
They aren't very friendly.
I don't know the answer.

They work hard.
John looks tired.
Janet came late to class.

George WAS angry, wasn't he!
I AM late, aren't I!
They AREN'T very friendly, are they!
I DON'T know the answer, do I!

They DO work hard, don't they!
John DOES look tired, doesn't he!
Janet DID come late to class, didn't she!

KEY VOCABULARY

ADJECTIVES

allergic	friendly
angry	generous
considerate	honest
cooperative	industrious
dedicated	nervous
efficient	online
engaged	overcooked
famous	pleased

polite
promoted
punctual
scary
shocked
sour
unfair
upset

NOUNS

accusation	memo
championship	moon
common cold	Olympics
couple	performance
cure	ride
dolphin	SAT test
engagement	score
guy	spare tire

spot
suspect
toaster
vacation day
wagon
wedding
anniversary
White House

VERBS

celebrate	observe
complain	perform
date	play frisbee
discover	skateboard
lock	star
mention	taste
miss	tie my shoes
move out	

Review:
Verb Tenses
Conditionals
Gerunds

- Invitations
- Expressing Disappointment
- Calling Attention to People's Actions
- Apologizing
- Giving Reasons

- Decision-Making
- Consequences of Actions
- Expressing Concern About People
- Asking for Assistance

VOCABULARY PREVIEW

1. cast	6. hamster	11. pet food
2. chicken pox	7. income tax return	12. satellite dish
3. cockroach	8. key	13. scrap paper
4. diner	9. mess	14. wallpaper
5. files	10. passport	15. wisdom tooth

Would You Like to Go on a Picnic with Me Today?

A. Would you like to **go on a picnic** with me today?

B. I don't think so. To be honest, I really don't feel like **going on a picnic** today. I **went on a picnic** yesterday.

A. That's too bad. I'm disappointed.

B. I hope you understand. If I hadn't **gone on a picnic** yesterday, I'd be very happy to **go on a picnic** with you today.

A. Of course I understand! After all, I suppose you'd get tired of **going on picnics** if you **went on picnics** all the time!

A. Would you like to _____ with me today?

B. I don't think so. To be honest, I really don't feel like _____ing today. I _____ yesterday.

A. That's too bad. I'm disappointed.

B. I hope you understand. If I hadn't _____ yesterday, I'd be very happy to _____ with you today.

A. Of course I understand! After all, I suppose you'd get tired of _____ing if you _____ all the time!

1. *see a movie*
   saw, seen

2. *go to the mall*
   went, gone.

3. *take a walk in the park*
   took
   taken

4. *work out at the gym*

5. *go bowling*

6. *have lunch at Dave's Diner*

7. *drive around town*
   drove, driven.

8.

How to Say It!

Invitations

Would you like to
Do you want to   } go on a picnic with me?
How would you like to

Practice the conversations in this lesson again. Invite people in different ways.

Do You Realize What You Just Did?!

A. Do you realize what you just did?!

B. No. What did I just do?

A. You just **ate both our salads**!

B. I did?

A. Yes, you did.

B. I'm really sorry. I must have **been very hungry**.
If I hadn't **been very hungry**, I NEVER would have **eaten both our salads**!

1. *throw out my homework*
think it was scrap paper

2. *drive past my house*
forget your address

3. *disconnect Aunt Thelma*
press the wrong button

4. *hit me with your umbrella*
be looking the other way

5. *step on my feet*
lose my balance

6. *give bird food to the hamster*
mix up the pet-food boxes

7. *paint the living room window*
have my mind on something else

8. *delete all my files*
hit the wrong key

9. *call me Gloria*
be thinking about somebody else

10. *put tomatoes in the onion soup*
misunderstand the recipe

11. *erase the video of my dance recital*
accidentally rewind the tape

12. *sit on my cat*
think it was a pillow

How About You?

Think of a time when you did something accidentally. What did you do? When did you realize what you had done? Why did it happen?

MARCIA'S BAD DAY

Marcia made several bad decisions yesterday.

She decided to drive to work, but she should have taken the train. If she had taken the train, she wouldn't have gotten stuck in a terrible traffic jam.

She decided to have lunch with a friend at a small restaurant far from her office, but she should have gone to a place nearby. If she had gone to a place nearby, she wouldn't have been an hour late for an important afternoon appointment.

She decided not to take the garbage out until after she got home from work that evening, but she should have taken it out in the morning. If she had taken it out in the morning, her cat wouldn't have tipped over the garbage pail and made such a mess in the kitchen.

And finally, that evening she decided to stay up late and watch a scary movie on TV, but she should have turned off the TV and gone to sleep. If she had turned off the TV and gone to sleep, she wouldn't have had terrible nightmares all night.

Marcia certainly didn't have a very good day yesterday. As a matter of fact, she probably shouldn't have gotten out of bed in the first place. If she hadn't gotten out of bed in the first place, none of this would ever have happened!

✔ READING CHECK-UP

TRUE, FALSE, OR MAYBE?

Answer True, False, or Maybe (if the answer isn't in the story).

1. Marcia wishes she hadn't taken the train to work yesterday.
2. If Marcia hadn't had lunch far from her office, she would have been on time for her appointment.
3. There aren't any small restaurants near Marcia's office.
4. She decided not to take the garbage out in the morning.
5. If Marcia hadn't watched a scary movie on TV, she probably wouldn't have had nightmares.

How About You?

We all sometimes make decisions we wish we hadn't made. Tell about some bad decisions you have made over the years. What did you decide to do? What should you have done? Why?

CHOOSE

1. If I _____ you were going to be in town, I would have invited you to stay with us.
   a. knew
   b. had known

2. If _____ busy tonight, I'll call you.
   a. I weren't
   b. I'm not

3. If I _____ the plane, I probably would have gotten there faster.
   a. had taken
   b. took

4. I _____ happy to go to the dance with you if you invited me.
   a. would be
   b. would have been

5. If I were you, I _____ that movie.
   a. wouldn't see
   b. won't see

6. I wish I _____ when I was young.
   a. learned to swim
   b. had learned to swim

7. If I had been more careful, I _____ driven through that stop sign.
   a. would have
   b. wouldn't have

8. I suppose you'd get tired of writing reports if you _____ reports all the time.
   a. wrote
   b. write

LISTENING

Listen and choose where the conversation is taking place.

1. a. restaurant
   b. someone's home

2. a. bus
   b. movie theater

3. a. park
   b. shopping mall

4. a. cafeteria
   b. supermarket

5. a. department store
   b. laundromat

6. a. airplane
   b. concert

You Seem Upset. Is Anything Wrong?

A. You seem upset. Is anything wrong?

B. Yes. **My computer is broken.**

A. I'm sorry to hear that. How long **has it been broken**?

B. **For two days.**

A. I know how upset you must be. I remember when MY **computer was broken**. Is there anything I can do to help?

B. Not really. But thanks for asking.

A. You seem upset. Is anything wrong?

B. Yes. _____.

A. I'm sorry to hear that. How long _____?

B. (For/Since) _____.

A. I know how upset you must be. I remember when _____. Is there anything I can do to help?

B. Not really. But thanks for asking.

1. My father is in the hospital.
   a week

2. My children have chicken pox.
   last Friday

3. The elevator in my building is out of order.
two weeks

4. My cat is lost.
three days

5. I'm unemployed.
March 1st

6. I'm having trouble sleeping at night.
a few weeks

7. Mr. Crump refuses to fix our bathtub.
a month

8. My wisdom teeth hurt.
Monday morning

9. My passport is missing.
I took an overnight train last week

10. The air conditioner in my office is broken.
the past week

11. I'm having trouble communicating with my children.
they became teenagers

12. My apartment has cockroaches.
a restaurant opened downstairs

Could You Possibly Come Over and Give Me a Hand?

A. Hello, Carlos? This is Gary.

B. Hi, Gary. How are you?

A. I'm okay. Listen, Carlos, I'm having trouble **putting up my satellite dish**. Could you possibly come over and give me a hand?

B. I'm really sorry, Gary. I'm afraid I can't come over right now. **I'm sick in bed**. If **I weren't sick in bed**, I'd be GLAD to help you put it up.

A. Don't worry about it. If I had known **you were sick in bed**, I wouldn't have called you in the first place!

A. Hello, _____? This is _____.

B. Hi, _____. How are you?

A. I'm okay. Listen, _____, I'm having trouble _____ing. Could you possibly come over and give me a hand?

B. I'm really sorry, _____. I'm afraid I can't come over right now. _____.

If _____, I'd be GLAD to help you _____.

A. Don't worry about it. If I had known _____, I wouldn't have called you in the first place!

1. *hook up my DVD player*

2. *figure out the math homework*

3. *move my piano*

4. *assemble my new bookcases*

5. *fill out my income tax return*

6. *set up my new computer*

7. *replace the lock on my front door*

8. *program my new cell phone*

9. *pick out new wallpaper for my kitchen*

10.

DECISIONS

Several years ago, Stanley's friends urged him not to quit his job at the post office. They told him that if he quit his job there, he would never find a better one.

Stanley didn't follow their advice, and he's glad he didn't. He decided to quit his job at the post office, and he found work as a chef at a restaurant downtown. He saved all his money for several years, and then he opened a small restaurant of his own. Now his restaurant is famous, and people from all over town come to eat there.

Stanley is glad he didn't listen to his friends' advice. If he had listened to his friends' advice, he probably never would have opened his restaurant and become such a success.

Kelly's parents thought she was crazy when she bought a used car that had already been driven over two hundred thousand miles. They told her that if she bought that car, she'd probably have lots of problems with it.

Kelly didn't follow her parents' advice, and she's really sorry she didn't. Since she bought the car two months ago, she has had to take it to the garage for repairs seven times.

Kelly wishes she had listened to her parents. If she had listened to them, she never would have bought such a "lemon"!

Jason's ski instructor insisted that Jason wasn't ready to ski down the advanced slopes at the Magic Mountain ski resort. She told him that if he skied down the advanced slopes, he'd probably injure himself.

Jason didn't follow his ski instructor's advice, and he's very sorry he didn't. He skied down an advanced slope, and after just a few seconds, he fell and broke his leg.

Jason wishes he had listened to his ski instructor. If he had listened to her, he wouldn't be lying in the hospital with his leg in a cast.

✔ READING *CHECK-UP*

TRUE, FALSE, OR MAYBE?

Answer True, False, or Maybe (if the answer isn't in the story).

1. Stanley's friends thought he shouldn't continue working at the post office.
2. Stanley is glad he followed his friends' advice.
3. Kelly's mother and father never buy used cars.
4. Kelly's car has been at the garage for repairs for seven months.
5. If Jason had listened to his ski instructor's advice, he wouldn't have skied down an advanced slope.
6. Jason hasn't had his leg in a cast before.

CHOOSE

1. If he _____ to their advice, he wouldn't have gotten hurt.
   a. listened
   b. had listened

2. Since I bought this computer six weeks ago, _____ take it to the repair shop three times.
   a. I've had to
   b. I had to

3. I'm sorry I _____ to my parents' advice.
   a. didn't listen
   b. hadn't listened

4. Sarah wishes _____ bought a used car from Ralph Jones.
   a. she hasn't
   b. she hadn't

5. If I _____ have to work overtime today, I'd be glad to go to the concert with you.
   a. didn't
   b. don't

6. If I _____ sick, I'd be happy to come over and help you.
   a. wasn't
   b. weren't

PRONUNCIATION *Would you & Could you*

Listen. Then say it.

Would you like to see a movie?

How would you like to go dancing?

Could you possibly come over?

Say it. Then listen.

Would you like to have lunch?

How would you like to go bowling?

Could you possibly give me a hand?

Write in your journal about a time when you had to make an important decision and people gave you lots of advice. What was the situation? What did people tell you? Why did they tell you that? Did you follow their advice? What happened? Do you think you made the right decision? Why or why not?

CHAPTER SUMMARY

GRAMMAR

REVIEW OF VERB TENSES
PRESENT TENSE: TO BE

My computer **is** broken.

SIMPLE PAST

You just **ate** both our salads.

PRESENT CONTINUOUS

I**'m** hav**ing** trouble putting up my satellite dish.

PRESENT PERFECT

How long **has** it **been** broken?
It**'s been** broken for two days.

SIMPLE PRESENT

I don't feel like going on a picnic today.

CONDITIONALS: REVIEW

If I hadn't gone yesterday, I**'d** be very happy to go with you today.
If I hadn't been very hungry, I NEVER **would have** eaten both our salads!
If I had known you were sick in bed, I **wouldn't have** called you.

GERUNDS: REVIEW

I don't feel like **going** on a picnic today.
I suppose you'd get tired of **going** on picnics if you went on picnics all the time!

KEY VOCABULARY

NOUNS

advice	income tax return	scrap paper
button	key	ski instructor
cast	mess	ski resort
chicken pox	passport	slope
cockroach	pet food	video
diner	pillow	wallpaper
file	repairs	wisdom tooth
hamster	satellite dish	

VERBS

assemble	press	save
delete	program	set up
disconnect	put up	tip over
erase	quit	urge
lose *my* balance	replace	work out
misunderstand	rewind	
mix up		

Volume 4   Number 4

Technology in Our Lives

Telephones then and now

Technology plays a role in all aspects of our lives—the way we work, the way we shop, the way we communicate with each other, and the way we live at home. The speed of technological change in the past one hundred years has been incredible.

The early telephones were very large, and they didn't even have dials or buttons. You picked up a receiver and talked to an operator who made the call for you. Nowadays, cellular telephones fit in our pockets, and we can use them to make phone calls from anywhere to anywhere. In grocery stores and supermarkets, cashiers used to punch keys on cash registers to enter the price of each item. These days, scanners read bar codes on product packaging, and the prices are recorded by a computerized cash register. In some supermarkets, customers can even check out by scanning products themselves and paying by credit card, all without the help of a cashier. In the past, we made a trip to the bank to deposit or withdraw money. Now we can use ATMs (automated teller machines) that are found everywhere. And many people now do their bank transactions at home online over the Internet.

Modern technology has dramatically improved our lives. Personal computers enable us to create documents, store information, and analyze data—at work or at home. The Internet allows us to send and receive e-mail messages, connects us to the World Wide Web, and allows us to go shopping online from our homes. Digital cameras enable us to take photographs that we can instantly put on our computers to store, change, and send over the Internet. Satellite communication connects doctors in one country with a patient in another country, bringing medical technology to remote places

around the world. Miniature cameras that patients can swallow permit doctors to diagnose medical conditions without surgery. "Smart homes" operated by computers turn lights on and off as people enter or leave rooms and enable homeowners to "call their houses" to turn on the heat or air conditioning, or even to start the coffeemaker!

What will the future bring? "Smart highways" will carry us to destinations that we program into our cars' computers. Computer chips that are implanted under our skin will hold our medical information in case of an emergency. Household appliances, such as refrigerators and stoves, will have miniature computers that "know" how we like to store or cook our food.

Many people feel, however, that technology has its price. With automated supermarket checkout lines, ATMs and online banking, and Internet shopping, we can meet our daily needs without having contact with other people. Life with technology can be very lonely! Also, many people are concerned about privacy. Technology makes it possible for companies or the government to monitor our use of the Internet. Our credit card numbers, bank account information, medical information, and other personal data are all stored on computers. Protecting that information will be an important issue in the years ahead.

Banking then and now

FACT FILE

Internet Users (in Millions)

Year	1995	1996	1997	1998	1999	2000

Technology in Action

Innovations in technology are happening throughout the world.

A satellite dish provides television service to a village in Niger in Africa.

Computer technology developed in Tokyo, Japan scans people's eyes to verify their identity.

A new type of scanner screens the baggage of airline passengers at an airport in Washington, D.C.

Solar batteries provide electricity for a hospital in Sudan.

Business people in Sao Paulo, Brazil take part in a video conference with people at another location.

An on-board computer enables the driver of this car to get maps and other information over the Internet.

A doctor uses tele-medicine technology to examine a patient in another country.

A grandmother uses e-mail to keep in touch with her grandchildren who live far away.

Are you familiar with any of these innovations in technology? Which ones? What other innovations in technology do you know about?

Interview

Q: How has technology changed your life?

A: With today's computer and information technology, I don't have to go to my office every day. I "telecommute." I can connect to the computer network at my company and work from home.

A: I love my new game system! The graphics are amazing, and the action is really life-like! When I grow up, I want to develop game system software.

A: I have three children and eight grandchildren, and they all live far away. I keep in touch with them through e-mail. They even send me photos over the Internet. Technology keeps our family together.

A: I use instant messaging all the time to stay in touch with my friends. I can have separate conversations with different friends at the same time over the Internet. It's better and cheaper than talking on the phone!

A: I don't know what I'd do without my cell phone! I'm never home, so I carry it with me everywhere. This way, my family and my friends can always reach me.

A: I have diabetes, so I have to monitor my blood sugar regularly. With my glucometer, I can check my blood sugar reading at any time of the day.

A: With my GPS device, I can navigate using global positioning satellite technology. It tells me the exact location of my boat at any moment.

FUN with IDIOMS

Do You Know These Expressions?

_____ **1.** There's a bug in this software!

_____ **2.** My computer has a virus!

_____ **3.** My computer is frozen!

_____ **4.** My computer is out of memory!

a. The system is infected.

b. There isn't space for more information.

c. The program has a problem.

d. Nothing is happening.

We've Got Mail!

Dear Side by Side,

    I have enjoyed using *Side by Side* in my English classes for the past two years. Now I'd like to ask for your advice. What is the best way for me to improve my English? Should I continue to study in school? Is there more grammar that I need to learn? What are some ways I can practice my English? I look forward to hearing from you.

Sincerely,

"Love Learning English"

Dear "Love Learning English,"

    We're happy to hear that you have been enjoying your English classes. In our opinion, you should definitely continue studying the language. There is more grammar to learn, and you will also be able to improve your listening, speaking, reading, and writing skills. In addition, try to use English as much as possible outside the classroom. Speak to people in English, watch English-language movies and TV shows, and try to communicate with people in English through letters or over the Internet. Thank you for writing, and good luck as you continue to study English!

Sincerely,

Side by Side

Global Exchange

Pop74: Hi, Sally. This is Grandpa. What's new?
CurlyGirl: NMU
  Pop74: ?
CurlyGirl: Not much. And you?
  Pop74: Grandma and I are fine. We loved the photos you sent us over the Internet of your Halloween party.
CurlyGirl: THX
  Pop74: ?
CurlyGirl: Thanks.
  Pop74: You looked great in your bee costume. Did you sting anybody?
CurlyGirl: LOL
  Pop74: ?
CurlyGirl: Laughing out loud.
  Pop74: Grandma says hello.
CurlyGirl: G2G ILU
  Pop74: ?
CurlyGirl: Got to go. I love you.
  Pop74: ILU2

Have an instant message conversation with a keypal. Talk about anything you'd like. Use some abbreviations in your message.

MORE ABBREVIATIONS

WU? = What's up?	OIC = Oh, I see.
UW = You're welcome.	IMO = In my opinion
L8R = Later.	TTYL = Talk to you later.

LISTENING

Thank You for Calling the Service Department

These people are calling the service department of the Supersonic Electronics store. Which person is going to press each number?

  _b_ **1** **a.** "When I try to play a video, nothing happens!"

  ____ **2** **b.** "I don't hear any sound in my headphones!"

  ____ **3** **c.** "Whenever I try to save my work, it freezes!"

  ____ **4** **d.** "All my photographs are too dark!"

  ____ **5** **e.** "I don't know how to record a message!"

  ____ **6** **f.** "When I call people, I can hear them, but they can't hear me!"

What Are They Saying?

Listening Scripts

Chapter 1 – Page 6

Carl is going to have a party at his apartment this Saturday night. This is the list of things that Carl needs to do to get ready for his party. Check the things on the list that Carl has already done.

Carl has already gone to the supermarket. He hasn't cleaned the apartment yet. He also hasn't gotten balloons at the party _____ some new dance music at his favor _____ _____ _____ _____tions yet. He a _____ abou _____ the _____ part _____

Ch _____

*Lis _____
co _____*

1. _____

2 _____

3 _____ 's

_____ ring

_____s and

_____ party.

_____e

_____nt. Your

_____ry. We've _____r is finally

_____e.

_____SB radio _____ist was _____erson Street _____he scene of _____olice _____e in the _____io News.

This is Kim Crane reporting live from City Hall. A new mayor has been elected. It was a very close race between Joe Murphy and Julie Miller, but now the results are in, and Julie Miller has been chosen as the new mayor. Julie Miller will be interviewed on this evening's news at six o'clock.

This is Stu Brent reporting live from downtown. I'm at the scene of the big fire at the Main Street Marketplace. Five stores at the Marketplace were destroyed in this fire that broke out early this morning. Luckily, no one was injured. The building is now being examined by the fire department. The fire chief is expected to speak at a news conference later this afternoon. We'll bring that news conference to you live when it happens.

This is Brian Adams with a local sports update. After five years as the city's baseball champions, the Washington High School Eagles were defeated by the Lincoln High School Terriers this afternoon by a score of 4 to 3. The Terriers are the new baseball champions. Tune in at 5 o'clock for the complete story.

This is Wendy Chen reporting live from the Museum of Fine Arts. Last night, the museum was robbed, and several important paintings were stolen. The paintings are considered some of the best works by painters known throughout the world, including Picasso, Rembrandt, and Monet. The robbery was discovered this morning when the museum's director arrived for work. The building is now being checked by the police, and information about the missing paintings is being sent around the nation and around the world. Reporting live from the Museum of Fine Arts, this is Wendy Chen for KPLW Radio News.

Chapter 4 – Page 61

Listen and decide where the conversation is taking place.

1. A. Could you please tell me if this book is on sale?
   B. Yes, it is.

2. A. Can you tell me where the bananas are?
   B. Yes. They're in the next aisle.
   A. Thanks very much.

3. A. Do you know how much this shirt costs?
   B. I'm sorry. I don't work here.

4. A. Do you know who composed this symphony?
   B. I think Beethoven did.

5. A. Do you by any chance know whether we'll be arriving soon?
   B. Yes. We'll be arriving in ten minutes.
   A. Thank you.

6. A. Who knows how a heart works?
   B. I do.
   A. Please tell us.

7. A. Do you know how much longer I'll have to stay here?
   B. Just a few more days.
   A. Oh, good.

8. A. Do you have any idea when the bus from Detroit arrives?
   B. I'm not sure. You should ask the man at the ticket counter. He'll know when the bus arrives.

Chapter 5 – Page 76

Listen and choose the statement that is true based on what you hear.

1. If it weren't raining today, we'd go to the beach.
2. If we had enough money, we'd buy a new car.
3. I'd be very happy if Mrs. Carter were my English teacher.
4. If the company's profits increase, we'll receive bonuses.
5. If I weren't allergic to trees, I'd go hiking with you this weekend.
6. If I didn't have to work tonight, I'd invite you to go to the movies with me.

Side by Side Gazette – Page 82

Listen to the Tempo Airlines automated telephone system. Match the numbers and the menu instructions.

Thank you for calling Tempo Airlines—the airline that puts passengers first! This call may be monitored to ensure quality assistance. Please listen carefully to the following menu:

If you are calling for information about today's flights, press 1.
If you are calling to make a reservation for a flight in the United States or Canada, press 2.
If you are calling to make a reservation for an international flight, press 3.
If you are calling to make a reservation for a Tempo Airlines Vacation Package, press 4.
If you are calling to enroll in the Tempo Airlines Frequent Flyer Program, which gives you awards for all travel on Tempo Airlines, press 5.
If you want to hear a list of rules for checking in at the airport, press 6.
If you want to speak with a customer service representative, press 7.
To hear this menu again, press 8.

If you are not calling from a touch-tone phone, please stay on the line and a Tempo Airlines representative will be with you shortly. Thank you for choosing Tempo Airlines.

Chapter 6 – Page 93

Listen and choose the statement that is true based on what you hear.

1. If I got a dog, I'd probably be evicted from my apartment building.
2. I wish I worked the day shift.
3. If I weren't a teacher, I'd probably be a musician.
4. I wish I didn't have to take biology next semester.
5. If I could type fast, I'd be able to get a better job.
6. If they lived in the city, they'd be able to sell their car.

Chapter 7 – Page 105

Listen and choose the statement that is true based on what you hear.

1. A. If I were rich, I'd travel around the world.
   B. Really? That sounds like fun!
2. A. Why didn't you e-mail me?
   B. I would have e-mailed you if I hadn't forgotten your e-mail address.
3. A. How did you enjoy the soccer game?
   B. It was all right, but I wish we could have had better seats.
4. A. Those boys are making a lot of noise in the hallway again.
   B. I know. It's terrible. If they weren't the landlord's children, I'd tell them to be quiet.
5. A. You know, I wish I had taken a computer course when I was in college.
   B. Why do you say that?
   A. If I had, I would have gotten the job I applied for.

6. A. Happy Birthday, Johnny! Now blow out the candles and make a wish.
   B. I wish Grandma and Grandpa were here for my birthday party.

Chapter 8 – Page 115

Listen and choose the statement that is true based on what you hear.

1. A. I've been in the office all day. I wasn't aware that it had snowed.
   B. I wasn't either.
2. A. Have you heard the news?
   B. No. What?
   A. Our supervisor is in the hospital.
   B. Oh. I didn't know that. That's too bad.
3. A. Do you know about the special sale?
   B. No, I don't.
   A. You can buy two jackets for the price of one this week.
   B. No kidding! That's great!
4. A. Hello.
   B. Hello, Tim? This is Barbara. I'm afraid I won't be able to have dinner with you on Saturday. I have to work.
   A. Oh. That's too bad.
5. A. Sherman quit his job!
   B. Really? What a surprise!
6. A. We've moved!
   B. Oh. I didn't know that. Where to?
   A. The other side of the town.

Side by Side Gazette – Page 128

Joe Montero is the office manager at his company. Listen to his voice mail messages. Why did each person call?

You have six messages.

Message Number One: "Hello. This is Jim Gavin. I'm one of the new employees on the third floor. I have a question. Why was three hundred and fifty dollars taken out of my paycheck? If you have time today, could you please call me at extension 45? Thanks very much." [*beep*]

Message Number Two: "Hi. This is Denise. I'm sorry, but I won't be able to go to the meeting this afternoon. I just found out about the meeting a half hour ago, and I have to pick up the boss at the airport. Let me know how the meeting goes." [*beep*]

Message Number Three: "Hi, Joe. This is Patty in Accounting. I see that you've just ordered one thousand pens for the office. I'm calling to let you know that we still have enough pens from our last order, so we won't need any more pens for a few more months. I've canceled the order. Okay? Thanks." [*beep*]

Message Number Four: "Hello. This is Jane Adams calling from the president's office. You told me yesterday that the painters would begin painting the president's office today, but they haven't arrived yet. Please let me know when they'll be here. Thank you." [*beep*]

Message Number Five: "Hello. This is George Johnson. I wanted to let you know that I won't be in the office tomorrow morning. I have to go to a doctor's appointment. If you need to talk to me, you can reach me on my cell phone at 881-595-7472. Thanks." [*beep*]

Message Number Six: "Joe? This is Michelle Mills. I really need to talk with you as soon as possible. I've been offered a job at another company, and I don't know what to do. I'd really like to stay here, but they're offering me a job with more responsibilities and a higher salary. Please call me back so we can set up a time to meet. Thanks." [*beep*]

Chapter 9 – Page 141

Listen and decide who is speaking.

1. A. I did well on my exam, didn't I?
   B. No, you didn't.
   A. I didn't?! I'm really surprised.

2. A. The mail isn't here yet, is it?
   B. No. Not yet.
   A. That's what I thought.

3. A. You've received our supervisor's memo, haven't you?
   B. Yes, I have.

4. A. You know . . . that suit looks very good on you.
   B. You're right! It DOES look very good on me, doesn't it!
   A. Yes, it does. I wonder if it's on sale.
   B. Let's ask somebody.

5. A. You were driving more than seventy miles per hour, weren't you!
   B. I guess I was. Are you going to give me a ticket?

6. A. I have some good news!
   B. What is it?
   A. You're fine. You can go home tomorrow.
   B. I can?!
   A. Yes, you can.
   B. I'm very glad to hear that.

Chapter 10 – Page 151

Listen and choose where the conversation is taking place.

1. A. Do you realize what you just did?
   B. No. What did I just do?
   A. You put too much pepper in the soup. Our customers will be sneezing all night!
   B. Oh. I'm sorry. I must have had my mind on something else.

2. A. I'm sorry. I must have thought this seat was mine.
   B. That's okay. Don't worry about it. I'm getting off soon anyway.

3. A. You know, I really don't feel like shopping today. Could we go someplace else and take a walk?
   B. Sure. That's fine with me.

4. A. What are you going to have?
   B. I'm not sure. If I hadn't had the chicken every day last week, I'd have the chicken.

5. A. Excuse me. You just put my shirts in your machine.
   B. I did?
   A. Yes, you did.
   B. I'm really sorry. I thought they were mine.

6. A. If I had known this was going to be so boring, I wouldn't have bought a ticket.
   B. I agree. I wouldn't have bought one either.

Side by Side Gazette – Page 162

These people are calling the service department of the Supersonic Electronics store. Listen to the service department's automated telephone system. Which person is going to press each number?

Thank you for calling the Supersonic Electronics Service Department. Our menu has changed, so please listen carefully to the following options:

If you are calling about a personal audio device such as a portable CD player, press 1.

If your call is related to a VCR or DVD player, press 2.

If you need assistance with a digital camera or video camcorder, press 3.

If this call is about a cellular phone, press 4.

If you are having a problem with a desktop computer or a notebook computer, press 5.

If you are calling about a telephone answering machine, press 6.

If you would like to speak to a customer service representative, press 7.

If you would like to hear these menu options again, press 8.

To end this call, please hang up.

Thank you for calling the Supersonic Electronics Service Department.

Irregular Verbs

be	was/were	been	leave	left	left
become	became	become	lend	lent	lent
begin	began	begun	let	let	let
bite	bit	bitten	light	lit	lit
blow	blew	blown	lose	lost	lost
break	broke	broken	make	made	made
bring	brought	brought	mean	meant	meant
build	built	built	meet	met	met
buy	bought	bought	put	put	put
catch	caught	caught	quit	quit	quit
choose	chose	chosen	read	read	read
come	came	come	ride	rode	ridden
cost	cost	cost	ring	rang	rung
cut	cut	cut	run	ran	run
do	did	done	say	said	said
draw	drew	drawn	see	saw	seen
drink	drank	drunk	sell	sold	sold
drive	drove	driven	send	sent	sent
eat	ate	eaten	set	set	set
fall	fell	fallen	sew	sewed	sewed/sewn
feed	fed	fed	shake	shook	shaken
feel	felt	felt	shrink	shrank	shrunk
fight	fought	fought	sing	sang	sung
find	found	found	sit	sat	sat
fit	fit	fit	sleep	slept	slept
fly	flew	flown	speak	spoke	spoken
forget	forgot	forgotten	spend	spent	spent
forgive	forgave	forgiven	stand	stood	stood
freeze	froze	frozen	steal	stole	stolen
get	got	gotten	sting	stung	stung
give	gave	given	sweep	swept	swept
go	went	gone	swim	swam	swum
grow	grew	grown	take	took	taken
hang	hung	hung	teach	taught	taught
have	had	had	tell	told	told
hear	heard	heard	think	thought	thought
hide	hid	hidden	throw	threw	thrown
hit	hit	hit	understand	understood	understood
hold	held	held	wake	woke	woken
hurt	hurt	hurt	wear	wore	worn
keep	kept	kept	win	won	won
know	knew	known	wind	wound	wound
lead	led	led	write	wrote	written

Thematic Glossary

repeat 82
replace 42
reply 126
report 50
require 43
reschedule 127
rest 122
retire 7
return 20
rewind 149
rewrite 41
ride 2
ring 79
rob 37
roll 89
run 4
run away 28
run by 98
run out of 99
run over 38
run up 28
sail 11
save 47
say 48
say hello 98
scan 159
scold 101
screen 160
search 99
see 3
seem 82
select 49
sell 9
send 6
serve 43
set 1
set off 99
set on fire 107
set up 1
settle 45
shake hands 15
share 92
shop 159
shout 74
shovel 22
show 49
shrink 99
shut down 99
sign 57
sing 2
sit 60
sit down 121
skate 22
skateboard 130
ski 29
skip 15
smile 23
sneeze 65
snore 7
snow 70
speak 1
spend 13
spill 47
splash 38
spoil 67
stand 38
stand out 125
star 135
start 11
stay home 17
stay up 67
stay 6
steal 38
step 149
sting 38
stop 13
store 159

strengthen 48
study 7
suppose 84
swallow 159
sweep 34
swim 1
swing 79
take 8
take a break 3
take a walk 27
take care of 26
take down 13
take in 41
take inventory 1
take lessons 103
take off 11
take orders 8
take out 35
take part 160
take up 47
talk 19
taste 137
teach 87
telecommute 161
tell 6
tell time 47
thank 40
think 21
throw 80
throw away 80
throw out 148
tie *my* shoes 135
tie up 49
tip over 13
train 12
transfer 49
travel 49
trust 97
try 28
tune in 50
tune up 42
turn 47
turn off 150
turn on 47
type 89
understand 26
urge 156
use 6
vary 126
verify 160
visit 27
vote 52
wait 7
wake up 13
walk 38
want 10
warn 122
watch 71
watch TV 17
water 47
water-ski 5
wear 4
weigh 62
win 18
wind up 22
wish 90
withdraw 159
wonder 20
work 7
work out 147
worry 26
worship 48
wrap 81
write down 114
write 1
yell 15

Ailments and Injuries
break 22
carsick 65
chicken pox 145
cold 22
common cold 135
diabetes 161
disease 99
flu 12
headache 20
heart attack 22
hurt 22
measles 60
sprain 55
stomachache 122
toothache 5

Animals
animal 43
beast 48
bee 38
bird 118
cat 87
cockroach 145
dinosaur skeleton 31
dog 6
dolphin 129
hamster 145
horse 2
lion 48
monkey 3
pet 79
poodle 31
puppy 109
tiger 48

Cars
auto 42
battery 42
brakes 42
bumper 42
car key 56
engine 42
gas 1
gas mileage 73
headlight 42
hood 42
license number 52
oil 42
radiator 109
spare tire 129
tire 42
used car 70
wheel 47

Clothing
clothes 18
jacket 132
jeans 17
pants 41
raincoat 91
shirt 86
shoes 73
suit 17
sweater 89
tee shirt 9
tie 132
tuxedo 4
umbrella 96
uniform 31
wallet 38
wedding dress 95

Computers and Technology
access 69
bar code 159

"bug" 161
computer 17
computer chip 159
computer network 161
computer system 6
computerized cash
register 159
desktop computer 162
e-mail 69
e-mail address 105
fax 6
files 145
game system software
161
GPS (global positioning
satellite) 161
graphics 161
home computer 47
information technology 39
instant messaging 161
Internet 69
Internet company 86
Internet shopping 159
key 145
memory 161
microchip 47
notebook computer 162
on-board computer 160
online banking 159
online 137
personal computer 159
printer 95
satellite communication
159
scanner 159
software 126
solar batteries 160
technology 159
tele-medicine 160
video conference 160
virus 161
website 125
World Wide Web 47

Describing with Adjectives
absent 57
advanced 17
afraid 76
aggressive 65
allergic 75
amazing 9
ancient 47
angry 25
annoyed 84
annual 104
another 21
anxious 60
automated 159
available 127
aware 42
awful 37
bad 22
beautiful 32
beginning 17
big 13
bored 143
brave 28
bright 80
broken 42
burnt 65
busy 6
cardboard 47
careful 72
careless 75
casual 125
challenging 125

cheap 70
clean 100
close 50
closed 70
colorful 33
comfortable 50
computerized 159
concerned 21
conditional 82
confident 42
confused 82
confusing 50
conservative 18
considerate 141
convinced 104
cooperative 141
correct 82
country 79
crazy 156
crowded 69
curious 21
current 125
daily 103
deaf 47
dedicated 141
delicious 33
different 48
difficult 92
disappointed 25
dressed up 65
each 80
easy 141
efficient 141
elaborate 48
electric 44
electrocuted 22
electronic 47
elegant 32
embarrassed 85
energetic 66
engaged 110
entire 17
every 116
exact 161
excellent 42
excited 113
exciting 39
exhausted 25
exotic 79
extra 127
falling 80
familiar 126
famous 44
fantastic 37
fascinating 33
favorite 48
financial 28
fine 42
firm 126
first 5
flat 118
folk 79
formal 126
former 115
frequent 82
friendly 68
frightened 24
front 42
frozen 161
full 80
full-time 83
funny 33
gas-powered 47
generous 137
giant 47
glad 37
global 50

good 18
great 13
green 79
handy 93
happy 37
hard 16
heavy 56
helpful 122
historic 44
honest 86
huge 48
hungry 79
hurt 28
important 27
impossible 79
impressed 49
impressive 33
incredible 9
industrious 141
informal 82
interested 49
interesting 33
international 39
irritable 28
jealous 85
large 18
last 17
late 20
life-like 161
light 80
little 24
live 50
local 50
lonely 28
long 80
long-distance 28
lost 15
low 103
lucky 28
mad 85
magnificent 33
major 47
manned 47
married 5
mass-produced 47
mean 28
mechanically inclined 93
medical 4
memorable 49
midtown 60
miniature 159
miserable 103
missing 62
modern 44
monthly 6
motivated 125
national 44
native 43
natural 49
nervous 74
new 3
next 70
nice 68
noisy 92
nosey 93
old 5
only 121
original 44
other 22
outdoor 13
out of order 153
outgoing 73
outstanding 50
overcooked 129
overnight 153
overseas 21
own 81

part-time 83
passive 50
perfect 135
personal 47
physical 73
pleasant 141
pleased 141
polite 122
political 33
poor 56
popular 70
positive 84
possible 79
pregnant 60
prepared 13
previous 18
professional 118
promising 49
proud 50
public 43
punctual 129
qualified 119
quality 82
quiet 121
rare 99
ready 6
rear 42
reassured 122
religious 48
remote 159
responsible 125
rich 70
right 20
rude 28
rusty 13
sad 33
same 125
satisfied 73
scared 28
scary 24
Scottish 47
self-conscious 93
separate 161
serious 121
several 44
shocked 138
short 32
sick 4
similar 80
simple 79
single 87
small 47
smart 71
soft 101
sorry 12
sour 137
spare 92
special 13
strong 72
stuck 15
sunny 66
sure 20
surprised 23
talented 136
tall 56
terrible 23
thoughtful 141
tired 8
true 12
trustworthy 126
unaware 115
unbelievable 9
understanding 28
unemployed 153
unexpected 100
unfair 140
unhappy 85

unlimited 47
unusual 127
upset 13
upstairs 111
used 70
vegetarian 5
visible 48
wet 105
willing 76
wonderful 13
wooden 47
worse 69
wrong 23
yearly 73
young 43

Describing with Adverbs

accidentally 38
accurately 141
actively 50
actually 26
again 50
almost 38
alone 114
already 6
always 13
appropriately 125
approximately 48
away 11
back and forth 142
badly 50
better 16
carefully 16
certainly 18
close 72
comfortably 19
commonly 50
completely 26
confidently 16
conservatively 125
definitely 18
differently 18
directly 126
downstairs 153
dramatically 159
early 13
enough 16
exactly 103
extremely 13
far 150
fast 16
finally 38
firmly 126
fortunately 28
grammatically 82
hard 13
high 48
honestly 125
however 13
indoors 13
instantly 159
instead 80
just 17
late 6
later 50
legibly 16
lightly 126
likely 125
loud 16
luckily 50
nearby 150
neatly 125
never 8
officially 44
often 19
on time 11

originally 79
particularly 70
past 148
patiently 60
physically 49
possibly 55
pretty 28
probably 6
quickly 13
quite 28
really 23
recently 4
regularly 161
shortly 60
simply 56
sincerely 50
slowly 137
so 24
softly 19
soon 16
still 13
through 22
totally 13
unfortunately 82
usually 24
very 6
well 13

Electronics and Media

answering machine 162
cable TV 45
camera 49
CD player 70
cell phone 8
compact disc 47
digital camera 159
DVD player 155
film 96
game system 161
headphones 162
personal audio device
    162
phone 15
photograph 33
portable CD player 162
radio 50
satellite dish 145
tape 149
telephone 39
television 47
touch-tone phone 82
TV 17
TV game show 77
typewriter 17
VCR 41
video camcorder 162
video 6

Events

accident 28
appointment 18
argument 25
audition 16
battle 48
birthday party 68
celebration 13
ceremony 11
date 122
dream 23
driving test 16
emergency 77
engagement 138
event 13
family trip 49
fight 48
hit-and-run accident 50
nightmare 150

opening day 44
party 6
phone call 28
picnic 82
race 50
robbery 109
safari 17
sale 104
space flight 47
space launch 11
town parade 89
trip 12
vacation 17
war 44
wedding 13
wedding anniversary 134

Family

aunt 36
brother 9
brother-in-law 115
children 9
cousin 29
Dad 20
daughter 12
family 13
father 115
grandchildren 71
grandma 20
grandpa 20
grandparent 5
great-grandchildren 71
husband 5
kids 155
mother 71
nephew 91
niece 111
parents 7
relatives 21
sister 5
son 4
uncle 33
wife 4

Food and Meals

baby food 83
beef stew 100
birthday cake 80
breakfast 10
cake 17
candy 121
casserole 31
cheese 52
chicken 80
cookie 16
corn 2
dessert 15
dinner 23
egg 53
fish 133
food 6
grape 80
hamburger 137
ice cream 130
ingredient 95
lunch 1
milk 137
nut 80
onion soup 149
pancake 10
peanut butter and jelly
    sandwich 10
salad 17
salt 67
sandwich 10
smoothie 9
soup 67

171

Index